Love in the Pancake Batter:
Notes From a Seat Beside the Floral Displays

Jo-Jo Tabayoyong Murphy

Dear Reader,
I hope my words
bring you comfort
and hope.
peace & love,
Jo-Jo

For dearest Mama

CONTENTS

Also by Jo-Jo Tabayoyong Murphy:

American Stew on Rice
Your Lunch Smells Funny
Bless This Bite

Unreal and Surreal
Recipe Optional
Sweet, Bitter, Pungent, Salty

Murphy Messages newsletter available on Substack.com

ACKNOWLEDGMENTS

It takes every bit of guts I can muster to publish my work.
I cannot present these books to the world without the encouragement of a
glittering inner circle.

My appreciation goes to my colleagues at the Westmont Public Library
Writing Factory, who have been my mentors since I began this crazy path.

I am grateful for all those souls who told me that they wanted to read
what I had to say about grief.

Thank you, Chris Kipp, Hank Duderstadt, Kathy Greidanus, Linda Mayor,
Linda Hehl Myers, Mary Horngren, and Padma Polepeddi for whispering,
firmly stating, and patiently inviting me to get this done.

I am grateful for my siblings, Wesley, Hazel, and Walter,
who shared Mama with me.

My daughter Aubrey, son-in-law Mike, and grrrand-dogs Riley and Raven
add sweetness and joy to my world.

As always, I declare my unending love for my husband Steve, who keeps me
alive and thriving with his delicious meals, neck massages, and diplomatic
responses when I ask whether I should keep doing this.

FOUNDATION

JO-JO TABAYOYONG MURPHY

WHY WRITE THIS BOOK?

Last August, Mama went on to the next life. As I faced the first Mother's Day without her presence, it was painful to see all the ads, stories, and gift items marketed toward this holiday. I told my husband that it was too hard to think of celebrating the holiday. He reminded me that I have a daughter. She wants to make the day festive for me. I deserve to be reminded that I raised a child who has added grace to our lives.

I put these pieces together to honor the amazing woman who brought me into the world. This is my final Mother's Day offering to her.

Among other wonderful skills, Mama was an excellent cook. She could feed four fussy offspring with very little notice and a handful of ingredients, infusing simple meals with rich flavor. Her table welcomed many strays, as my daughter called them. Anyone who was alone on special occasions was given an invitation to join the family feast.

Mama added her affection into everything she created. I have wonderful memories of holding up my blue bowl at breakfast time so that she could give me scrambled eggs and rice fried with garlic bits. My brother and I had our own small cake pans, which she would fill with batter and bake for us. There are those who say the secret seasoning to memorable food is love. That was Mama's main ingredient.

I share here Mama's final illness, passing, and what has come after that. Hopefully, my experiences will resonate with those of you who have also known great love and the transformation that comes from encountering unforgettable souls.

REASON TO CELEBRATE

"Mommy!"

How many of us hear that shrieked in a public place without turning to see whether our child is calling? My daughter is an adult and hasn't used that word in decades. Doesn't matter. I still look around in case she needs me.

My own Mama had four kids. I liken her job to that of a goat herder whose charges scramble over sheer rock cliffs, eat anything they find, and bleat constantly. How did she ever manage?

This weekend, our nation celebrates mothers. The ads have filled my email inboxes. Everywhere I go, shops and restaurants coax the public to remember that overworked, frazzled, exhausted parents deserve, need, and long for recognition. Woe to those who ignore or forget this holiday!

While I appreciate the sentiment behind such an outpouring of goodwill, I am a bit overwhelmed. Why should we do this only one day a year? What about those who miss absent mums? What if the person who raised you is not your mom? What if you just can't get behind the hoopla?

What if you feel you don't deserve praise and adulation?

I sometimes lacked confidence in my parenting abilities. Did I do something that would ultimately harm my child's psyche? How about the time I forgot to pick her up on time from preschool because I fell asleep? Why did I scold so much? Should I have made more money to help our family? Did I work too much?

The guilt and regret weighed me down.

Thankfully, other moms took the time to tell me everything would work out for the best. They assured me that there is no one right way to raise a tiny person. They reminded me that my intentions were loving. They showed me their grown offspring's before and after pictures. They said that I might enjoy each day more if I focused on the positives and forgave myself for the slip ups.

They told me my girl and I would survive the conflicts and reach a place where we got along as well as ever.

I held their words like a flotation device as I trod the waters of motherhood. I prayed, then prayed some more. I attended parenting classes. I filled the pages of endless journals with my thoughts but took the time to write at least five things each day that made me glad to be alive. That is how I made it through the years of being a stay-at-home mother.

When I see other parents struggle, I pay this favor forward. I try to let them know that their darlings are more resilient than pottery. Some of their most traumatic events will become family legends that make everyone laugh during holiday meals.

Also, their children may become parents themselves. When they do, they will develop a deep and abiding sense of appreciation as they understand the other side of the equation. Their mothers' words will fly out of their own mouths. Their perspectives will shift and they will give sincere thanks over and over.

Thank you, Mama.

May all of us parents enjoy beautiful Hallmark moments over the next few days. May we be surprised at random times during the year by other expressions of affection. May we forgive, reassure, and encourage each other for doing our best to nurture the ones who were placed in our care.

Happy Mother's Day, all y'all!

BREAKFAST ALL DAY

Mama made us *merienda* (the Filipino term for a snack) sometimes when we got home from school. One of my favorites was the plate-sized pancakes she would flip verrrrry carefully so that they would retain their astounding shape.

I remember admiring the white plastic Tupperware measuring cup when it was filled with gooey batter. There was enough rising powder to make the mixture fluffy. As soon as it hit the sizzling griddle, it would grow in height. Once the surface was covered in bubbles, I knew it was time to move it with a spatula.

I smothered my snack with butter and maple syrup. We didn't need a stack because one gargantuan flapjack was plenty.

My brother learned to cook Mama's recipe. He made my daughter many plates of cakes when she was young. She asked for them often.

I remember traveling to and from Dallas with my husband, sister, and Mama. We stopped at a Cracker Barrel restaurant along the highway one morning. As I watched Mama enjoy her breakfast platter, I understood where my affinity for this meal began.

The pancakes were perfectly made with crisp outer edges, chewy middles, and surfaces that absorbed the toppings well.

I saw smiles that mirrored mine as we gobbled up our platters of food.

Breakfast is my favorite order at a restaurant. It reminds me of having long conversations at late-night diners with people who make me laugh with abandon, waking up on weekends to the scent of milky flour frying in oil, and grinning at Mama as she carefully slid a griddle full of tasty goodness onto my plate.

JO-JO TABAYOYONG MURPHY

VIGIL

REACHING FOR SERENITY

When you feel stressed, what do you do to relax?

When worries start to shove their way into your stream of thought, how do you keep them from being bullies?

What helps you calm those frantic jumping beans of dismay?

I reach for coloring books, markers, and pencils. When my brain is occupied by decisions that are straining my ability to choose wisely, I opt to make easier choices. What shade makes a griffin's pointed tail stand out against a border? How might flowing waves be depicted in blue? Will a castle's flags need three or four contrasting stripes?

If even those simple decisions feel difficult, I sort objects. While clearing out my office, I gathered scads of binder clips. There were four distinct sizes. I was soothed by placing them in their own glass containers. This photo does not do justice to how tidy, colorful, and beautiful they look! My buzzing mind becomes quieter when I see those clips in order.

Our family has had a lot going on in the past few weeks. We have celebrated birthdays and my hubby's retirement. We have had a holiday. Tornadoes and growling storms have made us flee to the basement a few times. Extended family and friends have had concerns. Dentists, and doctors, and tests, oh my!

It's been enough to send this woman to a fainting couch!

Instead, I have listened to my favorite music, walked with my sweetheart's hand in mine, lounged in my comfy bed, cuddled grrrandpups, talked to kind souls, and meditated.

Every problem has a gift in its hands. Every time. Every single one. Without fail.

Sometimes the gift is oddly wrapped, but it is worth finding. Sometimes it comes hidden in a castle or metal clip.

August 1, 2023

PAIRS

Heavy topics. Serious issues. Emotions running high. Tears, raised voices, hearts beating loudly.

While I was on the phone at dusk, I looked at the big pine tree in front of our house. These two doves were canoodling while all this heightened energy was swirling around.

I felt calmer immediately.

A few nights ago, I spoke to someone who had gone through a similar experience. I asked how she endured the pain.

She told me that she relies on a solid core of loved ones. "If they are around, I know I will be okay."

Those words have been a lifeline.

I have survived some events that tore the heart right out of my chest. I have walked through bleak paths. I have felt as though peace might never return.

Eventually, every time, light returned. I laughed again. I pulled away from the shadows. I remembered that life is not always a stroll through the park, but I can keep walking through the rough sections.

As I healed, I heard a baby squeal with a delight that took over its entire body. I saw the moon rise and add a glow to my quiet neighborhood. I listened to a musician who interpreted a favorite melody in an entirely new arrangement.

I held my husband's hand and felt reassured.

Whatever comes, I will find the wherewithal to get through it. I will rely on my solid core of quirky, creative, pun-telling, treat-cooking, eloquent loved ones.

All will be well. Eventually.

August 4, 2023

COMPLETE

Little bits and pieces have filled in the grand design. Large anchor positions have been added. The border is sketched out. I know my reach, my depth, my boundaries, and my willingness to expand.

In other words, I understand the world I have built for myself.

There was a time I was a bit lost. There were moments when my dreams were clearly defined. There were versions of me that I probably would not recognize today. (I might not like some of them either!) I have been adding, releasing, transforming, and modulating this vessel in which my soul resides.

After all these decades, I have become fond of myself. Strange to come to that conclusion, but here I am.

I know I am flawed, but I accept those imperfections. I know I have limitations, but I also have figured out ways to overcome some of them. (After all, being five feet and a smidgen tall can determine a few restrictions.) I am learning fresh ways to maneuver through this planet every day.

It is a triumph to look directly in a mirror and see a likable person. That has not always been the case, so I am grateful for this level of self-awareness.

Hi, me! You are doing well. Keep going.

August 4, 2023

CONVERSATIONS ACROSS A TABLE

There are plenty of folks who ask how I am doing but are not eager to know the details.

There are a few people who will listen when I bare my deepest emotions. I can rant, chortle (what a great word!), make foolish jokes, speak until I get choked up, remember shared experiences, and gain insights when they do the same.

There are a handful of exquisite friends who will sit across a table and talk for endless hours, until we watch the sun travel across the sky, until we go from one mealtime to the next, until our phones buzz with texts/calls/messages asking where we are.

There are some treasured loved ones who can speak until they are ready to breathe deeply, leave the table, and face whatever situations have demanded their best, strongest, most devoted selves, while I do the listening.

I am fortunate to have a few kindred spirits in my circle who allow me to be myself. For them, I am truly grateful.

With them, I always leave every encounter feeling renewed.

August 5, 2023

NOW

In one small section of Costco, we saw Halloween costumes and a Christmas tree.

It is the beginning of August, my dears.

Outside, drizzles, grey skies, and a mild chill could have fooled us into thinking autumn was knocking on our doors.

August has just entered the year.

My hubby likes to plan. His lists include tasks for the next week, quarter, season, and year. He does not like surprises.

I like having unexpected wonders shake up my routine. A friend let me know he and his wife will be in town soon. Yay! Another dear couple planned a lunch with us that stretched into an afternoon-long, meaningful conversation. Ahhh. A song my honey likes finally became available on iTunes yesterday. What a treat!

Though my calendar is updated faithfully, I keep my schedule open for spontaneous miracles.

I have lived through enough shocks to understand that this very moment is all I know for sure. I love anticipation, but I do not let it pull my focus too far from what is happening in front of me.

Today, I felt peppy, slept enough to be energetic, had a great dinner with my best fella, and heard from a few good souls. I am grateful for all those gifts because I know they are not promised.

When I met a fluffy puppy the other night, I welcomed him every time he walked over for a cuddle. When the clouds streaked across a deep azure sky at sunset, I breathed that spectacle into my bones. When my friend told a witty pun, I laughed straight from my belly. When I sat with a container of ube ice cream, I savored every spoonful.

When I think of the many, many characters who have livened up my days, I cannot count all the ways they have affected my experiences. They have taught me how to wrestle a fitted sheet into a compact cube. They introduced me to the complex flavors of sushi. They ran to my side when I asked for saving grace. They talked and listened and advised and commiserated and picked up my daughter from school and showed me how to make a phrase more interesting and did not laugh when I got a poodle haircut and lent me a big serving platter and waited until I felt better during bouts of morning sickness and let me know I mattered.

Now. Here. Sincerely. Frequently. Grab this scene and draw all its magic into your heart.

Write that on your calendar.

August 7, 2023

SIMPLE LINES

If you could select the first image that others held of your face, what age would you choose?

If you only could only describe yourself in a short sentence, how would you capture your essence?

If a brief encounter with a stranger could make a lasting impact, how would you interact?

Consider the most recent conversation you had with someone you did not know well. Did you discuss frivolous matters, such as this steaming hot summer, a bit of gossip you heard about a celebrity, an observation you had on a recent movie, or the state of the crabgrass on a neighbor's lawn?

I speak to women as we wash our hands in restaurant bathrooms, especially if our eyes meet in the mirror. I find it interesting to comment on their quirky outfits or make a joke about the decor. It keeps the atmosphere light and friendly.

Sometimes, a two-minute chat can be revealing. One spoke of her exhaustion as she changed her wriggling infant's diaper. Another sighed as she adjusted her wig. She had just had a long round of chemotherapy. A young woman bubbled about her recent engagement. Her eyes could have illuminated the entire block!

Humans are pack animals. We are meant to travel the globe with others. We choose how many - or how few - to walk beside us. It can feel lonely and isolating when we are not able to share our thoughts.

I am most fascinated when I listen to others introduce another person.

"Hello, this is my college friend. We met while walking back to our dorm after a football game. Neither of us had paid any attention to the event. That bond has lasted forty years."

"I'd like you to meet my colleague. We have been side by side in three different companies. We can figure out solutions to complex issues while playing video games after work."

"This is my wife! She's in charge of our social schedule. I handle the cooking. We have learned to use our strengths."

How would you like to be remembered?

I hope others laugh or smile if my face comes to mind, even if our only encounter was over a couple of faucets at a fancy restaurant.

August 8, 2023

WATCHING THE HORIZON

Can you see the storm? Clouds above the trees are releasing an abundance of rain. Our car is heading in that direction, but the road beneath our wheels is dry.

For now.

If we catch up to the *Sturm Und Drang*, we will have to manage whatever comes.

Have you ever had situations like that? Possible horrors, torments, wicked creatures, and furies writhe in the future. Whether they will arrive is uncertain. When they will manifest is not promised.

The dread can be paralyzing.

We might devote our energies toward devising solutions, creating barriers to protect us, or hiding. In the weeks, days, hours, and eye blinks before Zero Hour, we whip ourselves into a frenzy.

What a tremendous waste of our lives.

So many monsters I have imagined never knocked on my window. So many pitfalls never materialized. So many zits never bloomed on my nose before an important performance. So many trains, alarm clocks, opportunities, and prizes were right on time!

Have I been defeated? Oh yes, many times saw me on the losing side. Have I failed? Um, I have done so on a well-lit public stage. Have I gotten wounded? Do you want to see or hear the litany of my scars?

Despite those colossal upsets, I am still here. I must be a Weeble because I get knocked over, but I spring back up. (Non-Boomers may have to Google that reference!)

I may be facing some wretched patches, but I will not spiral into dismay. I have confidence that I will prevail because history shows that I have done so in the past.

I keep hoping, praying, visualizing, and yearning for positive outcomes. I keep aiming for the other side of the storm.

August 9, 2023

ANNIVERSARY

Tossing us back to a party at my parents' home. I don't know the occasion, but I know it was some sort of celebration because there was a decorated cake on the table.

My family loves to cheer around some frosting!

August 16th will mark 65 years since their wedding day. My dad left us after their 45th anniversary. My mom has missed him terribly ever since.

I'm grateful for this sweet memento of their affection for each other.

August 9, 2023

LEADING LINES

Photographers use leading lines to point toward focal points. For example, this scene has a lighted sidewalk on the left drawing your eye toward the back. The traffic lights mimic the pattern of the clouds. The tree line echoes the dark cumulus figures. The street has painted paths that divide the scene between colorful areas and taupe pavement.

I could exaggerate and say that these lines were intentional, but I won't. It took several tries to get this shot.

We were having dinner with friends when I noticed this dramatic sunset. The light, shadows, and brilliant hues changed from minute to minute. When I mentioned it to everyone, one friend jumped from his chair to take some pictures. I was inspired, so I ran outside, too!

I'm grateful all of us were able to gape at this phenomenal sunset. It was a gift for each one at the table.

As cars passed me on the street, I wondered whether any of the passengers noticed what was happening above them. I hope they did!

The show became muted only minutes after this. If we had ignored it or waited too long to react, we would have missed the magic.

This has been an emotional week. A night of talking to dear friends, sharing delicious food, and standing in awe together has given me a much-needed shot of positive energy.

Always follow those lines that point to magnificence.

August 10, 2023

HOMECOMING

Tossing us back to my dad's hometown, Laoac, Pangasinan, Philippines about 63 years ago. Mama is the lady framed by the doorway. My dad's sisters, sister-in-law, and cousin joined us on the front steps. Behind the banister on the left is my dad, I think.

Look at all the fresh, young faces, pretty dresses, and elegant postures that were captured here!

I wish I could join them all again on the porch on a sunny afternoon.

#tossingusback

P.S. Please say a prayer or keep a good thought for my Mama. She is having some serious health issues.

August 11, 2023

FEATURES, OPTIONS

When a car is designed, there are factory-made components, the basics. A buyer sometimes has the chance to choose a color, select upgrades, or add personal touches. These can be made before or after the purchase.

There are also specific parts that make one vehicle part of a brand. For example, a Rolls Royce can be custom-made to fit the owner's body measurements. When it rolls off the assembly line, it will have the RR emblem, no matter how uniquely built it is.

If I look in a mirror, I can spot the mole on my forehead, a scar from an injury, and worry lines. Those are the results of my individual development.

I can also recognize expressions I picked up from my parents, bone structure that came from my grandparents, and weak eyes that came from my ancestors.

Previous generations survived wars, famines, diseases, and natural disasters. They gave birth in trying circumstances. They buried many young children. They sacrificed to keep their families fed and sheltered. They taught their offspring how to take care of themselves.

Hundreds of years later, all those conditions, efforts, random occurrences, and good fortune produced my parents, who then collaborated to create me.

What are the odds, eh?

You may believe that nothing happens by chance. Or you may float through life feeling that everything is unpredictable or spontaneous.

Either way, here I am expressing these thoughts. Here you are, reading my words. Here we are connecting for an instance in a vast universe.

Staggering, isn't it?

August 11, 2023

SCANNING THE HEAVENS

I have written dozens of sentences and erased them. A few taps of my backspace key and those clumsy phrases are forgotten. I have so much to share, but feel inadequate to make it comprehensible.

I long to describe dread that can sap your legs of the energy to move toward a scene that could crack your heart into fragments.

I want to tell you about the life-giving sap that drips from prayers spoken on behalf of another, the entreaties laid at the feet of God asking for succor, and familiar litanies that remind us of other harrowing experiences that we survived.

I witnessed gentle, affectionate actions that eased pain, conveyed empathy, and brought solace.

My brother played simple tunes on a ukulele that coaxed a song out of my mom's parched lips.

My sister firmly guided my mother's ailing form in the gentlest ways.

Another brother held Mama's hand until her agitation eased.

My cousin shared her nursing expertise to give us clarity and prepare our hearts for what comes next.

A friend quietly bustled around us, washing dishes, picking up necessities, giving hugs, and doing a myriad of tasks that made the day go more smoothly.

My husband helped us get nourishment when we forgot to eat.

Another dear soul surprised us with a visit. Her radiant smile and soothing presence lightened our spirits.

A hospice nurse patiently explained intricacies until we could understand and accept them.

Two pastors visited and witnessed my parent's assurances that she knew who was leading her from this life to the next.

Another cousin brought us reasons to laugh, remember sweet times together, and strengthen our bonds to a family that extends around the globe and beyond this earthly realm.

FaceTime, text, voicemail, phone calls, and social media posts transported love, prayers, good wishes, smiles, offers of assistance, and tears into our presence from those who wanted to join our vigil somehow.

I sat in a quiet, darkened room. I counted my mother's breaths. I felt a howl rise from my belly, which was reduced to a few sobs so that I would not frighten crows from the trees.

Perhaps the sky senses our turmoil and translates it into clouds that grow into cosmic mountain ranges. Maybe light carves an opening that gives light a pathway through the shadows. The deep black night sky may shove all the clouds away so that the moon has a solo stage or, in the case of this weekend, so that thousands of shooting stars may grant wishes.

What are the odds, eh?

You may believe that nothing happens by chance. Or you may float through life feeling that everything is unpredictable or spontaneous.

August 12, 2023

SAVING A PLACE

A friend made this pillow for me. The message is brief. Its impact is timeless.

Some cultures have a tradition of having an empty chair at the table during special occasions. They reserve a spot for those who are no longer with us in this realm but will always have a place in our hearts.

Mama is approaching the gates of Heaven slowly, in her own time. When I left her last night, I kissed her forehead. She signaled that she wanted to kiss me, too. That broke my heart wide open.

At her weakest and most vulnerable point, she still manages to let us know she loves us.

I left her home tonight and kissed her again, but she was sleeping. I didn't want to wake her.

Many dear people came to visit Mama today. They have known and loved my mother for years - some for longer than I have been alive!

They will help us hold the best memories of my family.

We humans comfort each other during times of crisis, providing lifelines, listening ears, hugs, food, and acts of service. We guide each other through the dark tunnels that we have traversed before, letting our friends know that we have seen the end of the frightening section. "It's up ahead. We will get there soon, arm in arm."

Those who have been wounded have scars where those hurts were healed. Those signs of endurance give the rest of us hope. We know that we can be at peace again, maybe not today, but some day.

The empty chair is there for us to invite others to join the celebration, whether they live here or in our sweetest recollections.

Sit down. We are glad you are with us, giving hugs, and doing a myriad of tasks that make the day go more smoothly.

August 13, 2023

APOLLO'S ORBIT

I witness the first blush of morning, stars giving center stage to a closer, more flamboyant light source.

Even on a grey, drippy, yawn-inducing kind of dawn, the illumination changes.

At dusk, players switch roles. Subtle sparkles take over for their glowing sister.

The wild woman moon disregards this arrangement by appearing like a second sun on a summer afternoon or outshining those humble constellations when their shift begins.

I look at the seasons of a person's life like the back and forth of sky characters. We arrive, sail through our arc, then depart like Apollo on his chariot. During that journey, unexpected events divert us from a smooth path.

Triumph, tragedy, first love, new shoes, disappointment, the taste of a lime popsicle, learning how to decipher words on a page, hearing a devastating prognosis, discovering superpowers, watching a child receive a prize, and creating something from one's imagination add zest, teach us, and make the journey worthwhile.

As we travel along the way, we pummel each other. We bind wounds with gentle care. We argue over nonsense. We cradle the injured. We gleam with kindness. We tarnish with bitterness. We develop into our full-bloom magnificence.

As I watch carefully and wait for my mom to take that last curve below the horizon, I trace the events on her arc. She has been a beloved youngest granddaughter, daughter, sister, aunt, cousin, wife, mama, neighbor, volunteer, and nurse. Even during her last days with us, she struggles to communicate, focuses on conversations, looks straight at us, and greets us by name.

It occurred to me that she may be like our sun. When she disappears below the horizon on my hemisphere, she may be rising in another dimension.

I will try to keep that in mind when I miss her. She will be glowing in another sky, waiting for me to traverse my own trail. Then, we will be together again.

Meanwhile, I watch her blanket rise and fall with each breath.

August 14, 2023
1:48 a.m.

LOVE IN THE PANCAKE BATTER

EL FIN

My mom passed at 11:59 a.m. this morning. I know where she is now, and I am at peace.

I love these photos of Mama, me, and my daughter because they show that her genes have contributed to our personalities and beliefs.

Throughout my life, we had a bond. We clashed, we contrasted, we had times of separation, but I know she was always, always part of my blood, bones, heart, and outlook.

Before she left, I had a few minutes alone with her. I asked her forgiveness for any of my shortcomings. I told her I also forgave her everything. All I would remember would be love.

All that remains is the love.

Enjoy your welcome party, Mama! We love you!

August 14, 2023

SEND-OFF

OBITUARY

Gel, to friends and family, was born on February 2, 1932, in Ilagan, Isabella, Philippines to the late Tomas and Mauricia Altamero. She grew up in Solano, Nueva Vizcaya. Gel met her husband in 1953, the late Wesley T. Tabayoyong, M.D., with whom she would share 50 happy years until his death in November 2003. They loved welcoming guests into their home to worship, make music, and share feasts. Gel's cooking was legendary. Her natural gift for languages made her a valuable interpreter. She was outgoing and made friends easily. She was highly intelligent, finishing her nursing board exams at 4th place overall, and was once presented a scholastic award by First Lady Eleanor Roosevelt.

Wesley and Gel ran a family medical clinic for many years. Their patients spanned many generations. As a nurse, Gel cared for countless babies with gentle, loving expertise, her favorite being newborns.

Evangline poured her heart into raising her children, Jo-Jo (Steven) Murphy, Wesley II, Hazel (Tom Biagi), and Walter. She is also survived by her granddaughter Aubrey (Michael) Fitzner.

She had a deep, unwavering Christian faith, was a dedicated nurse, and had a strong devotion to her family. Her children and granddaughter were her pride and joy. She had a powerful soprano voice that choirs depended on to hit the high notes.

She was preceded in death by her siblings, Esther, Ruth, Tomasa, Paul, Ernest, George, Edwin, and Jose. She is survived by her brother, Tomas Altamero, Jr. Gel was a fond aunt of many and dear friend to all.

ONLY LOVE REMAINS

I was my mom's first child, the practice kid, the one who gave her a lot of grief, and the one who tried to be her back-up with my siblings.

She knew me well. I could depend on her when I was ailing because she was the best nurse I have ever known. When I had surgeries, she stayed with me in the hospital. She took care of my daughter for several years so I could work. She fed me and anyone else who entered her sphere.

She took care of our family after my dad passed almost twenty years ago.

We have been fortunate. In the past few years, Mama survived a heart attack, Covid, several bad injuries, and the heartbreak of selling her home. She endured, mostly for the sake of her four children and granddaughter.

At 91-and-a-half, she was still a force of nature. She and her sisters lived past their 90th birthdays. My Auntie Esther had her 101st birthday! We thought she had another ten or fifteen years left.

I woke up to a vision this morning. I saw cumulus clouds glowing with bright colors, like these from tonight's sunset. A crowd could be seen silhouetted against them. Though I opened and closed my eyes a few times, turned to my right and left, I kept seeing sections of that scene. Details that stood out were someone holding many balloons, a simple empty wooden cross, and then, after several views, my dad sitting at an upright piano. I realized I was given a peek at the welcoming crowd that awaited my mom in Heaven.

I jumped out of bed and ran to tell my husband we needed to leave in a few minutes so that we could see my mom.

He was astonished but knew after 38 years of marriage that he needed to do what I asked.

Thank God I listened to my instincts. We made it in time to say our goodbyes before my mom went to that festive reunion in Heaven.

Mama left while my brothers, sister, and I held her, told her how much she was loved, and reassured her that we would be fine on our own.

We have heard from so many in our loving circle today. Friends of my mom who have never met me stopped to describe how she affected their lives. I know we will hear more great stories in the coming days.

I wish I had a polished, elegant portrait with Mama, but I do have this memento of a visit eleven days ago when she was able to joke, listen to our tales, and enjoy having her family around. Even though she slowly became too weak to do simple things, I have decades of memories to relish.

I have been imagining all the hugs, shouts of delight, four-part harmonies, and beaming smiles she is enjoying in Paradise. Mama and Daddy must be thrilled to celebrate their 65th anniversary together.

I am the eldest child of Evangeline, my dear Mama.

LAST RIDE

Tossing us back with a family photo from 1965. We took a long road trip to the East Coast. My youngest brother turned five months old as we crossed a bridge into New York City.

My intrepid young parents bundled the four of us in a Chevy Nova and followed my more-experienced uncle and aunt on interstate highways across the country.

I was six years old. Everything looked impossibly grand! When I consider the places we saw, I was not wrong. We explored highlights, such as Niagara Falls, the Liberty Bell, the Statue of Liberty, the United Nations building, and Radio City Music Hall.

Mama was so chic and slender after giving birth to four children in about six years! How did she have the patience and strength to raise four of us rascally rabbits?

I am bracing myself for today. Mama's wake is this afternoon. We will begin saying farewell.

I'd rather take her on a long drive through the countryside.

FAMILIAR SOUNDS

I heard my mother's voice for the first time when I was growing in her belly. I'm sure she hummed and laughed and sang and spoke to tiny me often during my incubation period.

Today, my sister played some videos she had taken of my mom over the past couple of weeks.

As I listened, Mama's timbre, low chuckle, cadence, and expressions were so familiar. She sang a few songs in her lilting soprano. She could have been in the next room!

I began sobbing, something I rarely do.

I realized that these sounds have been in the background most of my life. They truly were my first audio experiences.

Now, their absence will reverberate for the rest of my life.

IMPRESSION

When we had a house blessing, my parents prepared a concrete slab so that all of us family members could sign our names, leave hand- and footprints, and be photographed doing it. I believe we had visited Los Angeles and seen the famous Grauman's Chinese Theater collection.

My daughter inherited the memento a while back. Today, I tried to see whether my hand was close to Mama's size. I fit her impression perfectly. I checked and found that my handprint had not changed from its original size back in 1973. Mama and I were the same!

This shocked me because I had been holding her hands a lot over the past few days. Her fingers had become very slender. She could not really squeeze me back any longer. I thought she had been a more delicate and diminutive size.

How will my memories of her change now that she has gone? Will she seem larger than life? I can recall her voice easily. Will I ever forget it?

Many have told me stories of relationships with my mother from various eras in her life. My cousins adored her. Co-workers respected her acumen. Neighbors enjoyed her warmth. Friends each felt they were her bestie.

Each encounter left an impression.

Mama was not one to have a heavy stride, but she left indelible footprints whenever she walked beside someone else.

51

GEL'S GARDEN

At Mama's wake and my home, floral arrangements began to arrive this week. No two were alike. Each one represented a person or group of people who loved my mom or her children.

Mama adored growing things, especially flowers. If I had a plant that was ailing, she could revive it. A yellow, scraggly, dejected looking specimen would suddenly thrive! If I checked on it a few weeks later, I could not recognize it. After that, it felt cruel to take it back because it had fallen in love with Mama.

We asked folks to tell stories about their experiences with our mom during tonight's wake. Oh my! We were entertained, fascinated, awed, and surprised by the tales. Occasionally, I cried. More often, I laughed until I made that raspy sound of my insides shaking with delight.

Mama's circle was as varied as these floral tributes. We heard from co-workers, church friends, neighbors, and dear ones who had known her for decades. The theme that was threaded through these recollections was Mama's ability to make others feel recognized, appreciated, unique, and welcomed.

I am both exhausted and energized. After getting only 4-1/2 hours of sleep, my battery needs charging, yet my mind keeps reliving the special moments of today.

Relatives and friends flew and drove here from other states and another country. My daughter and son-in-law watched from their vacation spot in

Italy. We felt love, prayers, and support. They kept us going on one of our most emotional days. The hugs I got were like shots of the purest vitamins.

After we left the funeral home, a few of my relatives came to my house. My cousin treated us to Lou Malnati's pizza! My mom's dear friend gave us delicious pasta. Other wonderful ones gave us a huge stack of muffins.

We gobbled, told jokes, shared stories, and enjoyed sitting around a table with others who adored Mama, including my uncle, her last remaining sibling. It was a reunion for the record books!

In a few hours, I will wake up and prepare to say goodbye to Mama's earthly remains. We have planned a service of prayers, scripture readings, songs, and messages. My siblings and I will give tributes. Then, we will lay Mama to rest beside Daddy.

I had a few minutes alone with my mom this afternoon before everyone arrived. That felt both sacred and ordinary. I will be talking to Mama and sending messages to the skies now. There are no more barriers, limits, or restrictions on where she can go. She and my dad can be with all our family members simultaneously if they would like. How cool is that?

Mama's garden of loved ones flourished. She added new varieties of souls often. Under her gentle care, every one of them grew into a prize-winning specimen.

Thank you, Mama.

RELEASE

Filipino funerals can be intensely emotional. In my experience, it is not uncommon to sob, roar with laughter, sit up with surprise, have a revelation, or feel the presence of angelic beings during an hour-long service.

This is the only photo I took during Mama's funeral. The rest of the time, I was sitting in the front row, speaking, listening, and crying. No interest in using my camera.

Shocking, right?

This image captures so many of the details that made the past two days so profound.

The woman on the far left was one of our funeral directors. Laurie and other staff members helped us photocopy music, answer logistical questions, arrange flowers, calm down enough to endure the chaos, and care for Mama.

My sister is the one taking a picture. She wore one of Mama's beaded Filipino tops today.

My two brothers are the front pallbearers. Steve, Tom, and four cousins were the other pallbearers.

I snapped a quick shot as I stood in front of a first-row chair at graveside as Mama was carried there. My siblings joined me. We sat in birth order.

Pastor Edwin led the service. As he gave the homily, he spoke of Mama in a way that showed he knew, respected, and loved her. In my head, as a prayer, I said thanks many times that he was able to officiate both services. He was the one who prayed in Mama's ear during the last minutes of her life. After he gave the Benediction, she took a final breath. That showed us she could hear and comprehend everything that was said to her until her eyes opened in Heaven. She listened to all our words of farewell, love, and caring.

My sweet niece played the piano for our service. She did so at short notice, yet fulfilled her duties with grace, skill, and patience.

My husband and two cousins read the Scriptures so well! Their words were measured and clear. Familiar verses seemed to take on fresh meaning.

My siblings and I gave our tributes in unique, individual ways. I read two of my poems as I spoke about Mama. My brother described his experiences as her roommate over the past 18 years and shared the story of when my parents met. He told us Mama's message that "God is in everything." My sister sang a poignant and beautiful song she composed for Mama that made me weep as I held the lyrics in front of her guitar. She had never been able to play it for Mama. I am in awe of her ability to finish the song while crying. She even managed gorgeous harmonics! My youngest brother's tribute made us both laugh with gusto and tear up. He had the congregation spellbound. He skillfully sang a song my dad composed for my mom before they were married, joined by a few other loved ones. I hope our parents were watching us together. I think they were proud of what we did. I loved every moment of our eulogies because they demonstrated how our folks encouraged us to be our truest selves.

Once again, we ended with the Seven-Fold Amen. This time, I allowed the rich harmonies and strong voices to inundate my being. I looked at my mom's face as we sang and wished her Godspeed.

The room was filled with people who shared moments with Mama and wanted/needed/went to great lengths to pay their respects this week. Some big families were represented by one member. They carried the prayers and good wishes of their tribes. Loving hearts made them hop on overseas flights, drive for hours through many states, squeeze in part of the services between wedding preparations, beg for time off work, walk in with canes or crutches, and rearrange their lives to be at our side.

Several told me they had returned from vacation just in time to be there. They heard about the events through word of mouth, Facebook, Pony Express, or divine intervention. I even got the time wrong when I announced it yesterday, but everyone still made it.

We ran about an hour late. Maggiano's banquet staff waited patiently. We got a bigger room than anticipated! The food was abundant and delicious. I felt as though Mama threw all her special souls a great party as she said goodbye.

Some family members dropped by our home afterwards. Our bellies were full. Our hearts were soothed.

It was awesome to hear our walls ring with joyful conversation, loud guffaws over old jokes and new tales, and the other sounds that happy people make

56

when they are among those who love them.

Our grrrand dogs have been patient with us. They have been helped by dear ones while Steve and I have been tending to funeral activities. We were greeted with wagging tales and welcoming barks tonight.

I did not know how I would react as we laid our mother beside our father for eternity. I can honestly report that it was one of the most uplifting, heartbreaking, and healing experiences of my 64 years. I had to make quick decisions, cooperate with my siblings, craft speeches about personal relationships, remember to eat and drink and go to the bathroom and sleep, convey overwhelming gratitude, offer hospitality the way my mom always did, all while knowing I would never see Mama's eyes look at me with love ever again.

I have had easier months, but I have never grown as much as I have in the past three weeks.

ANODYNE

My parents are together again. They met seventy years ago. My dad was besotted that day. He told her he could not wait to see their four cute future children.

He was certain and very forward to say such a thing to a relative stranger.

They were a matched pair for fifty years. After my dad went ahead, Mama waited almost twenty years to join him.

She never stopped missing him. Tradition says a surviving spouse must wear black for at least one year. Three years after he died, she surprised us by wearing something that was a pale pink shade to my daughter's graduation.

Until then, black had been her singular motif. It was glorious to see the color return to Mama's world. Now, I am imagining the brilliance of her smile as she reunited with that bold lad who won her heart.

GENTLE ARMS

When your knees cannot be counted on to keep you upright, who lends you strength?

When you cannot remember whether you have eaten or had any liquids in several hours, who fills your plate and cup?

Who reminds you of the greatest jokes, the sweetest celebrations, the best triumphs, and the times you prevailed over trials?

Who tells you, "We would not have missed this!" and actually shows up?

Whose bonds are strongest when you need lifelines?

These are a few of the amazing members of our circle who drove, flew, made their way with canes in hand, and kept us going. I could have filled page after page of photos but wanted to give a glimpse of our loving crew.

These are some of our angels.

HOUNDS HEALING HEARTS

August began with such promise. My hubby retired at the end of July. We were keeping our calendar open. Anything might happen. Oh, the anticipation was delicious.

On August 4th, my mom began having hospice care. By August 14th, Mama opened her eyes in Paradise. On August 18th, we laid her to rest beside my dad.

I have not yet caught my breath.

Riley and Raven, our grrrand-pups, have been my shadows. They seem to sense my need for consolation.

Raven weighs 80+ pounds. (For you metric folks, that is the rough equivalent of a 12-year-old child who enjoys snacking.) She tried sitting with me on a recliner, but I could not balance the two of us. I moved to the couch and Riley raced to get the spot closest to my head. Raven did her best hangdog pose when she lost her optimal position.

As I write this, the two of them have curled up on both my lap and beside me. I feel so protected.

Does an injured heart have a fragrance that alerts pets?

Do our animal companions sense what human brains and logic cannot accept?

There are no better ambassadors for calling home a heart that is drifting further and further from home. There may be other methods, but I like this prescription for a cold heart: take two snuggly dogs and allow them to make you warm, comfortable, and happy.

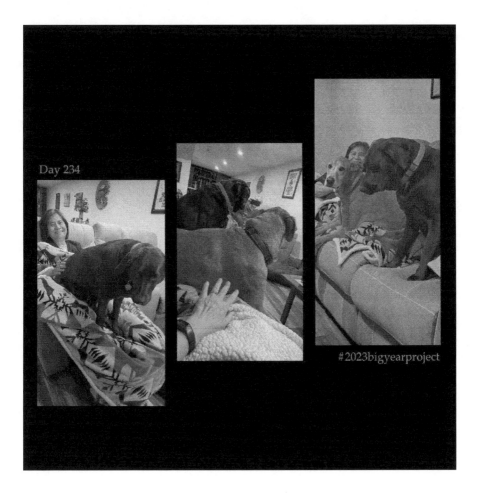

FEELINGS, FLAMES, FERVOR, FRIENDS

If you had a long evening to spend chatting around a fire pit, who would get a chair beside you?

My circle of loved ones has kept me and my family from faltering during this past month. I am grateful for every caring soul.

I am giving myself a night off, so this poem is an old favorite of mine from a few years ago. It fits that feeling of being carried by affection.

August 22, 2023

"Turn on the Porch Light"
by Jo-Jo Tabayoyong Murphy
Copyright May 9, 2016

Cocktail parties or family barbecues in the backyard?
Give me a fire pit and comfy flannel clothes!
Glamour and glitz or cocoa and ottomans?
Hold the sparkle, heap on the warmth.
Let me be around the ones who beam when I appear.
Keep me from those whose grins never reach their eyes.
The few I truly love deserve my attention.
I will give my precious seconds and energy to those who come first,
not the ones who do not know my favorite flavors.
Share a bawdy joke with me that makes me laugh until I can't breathe!
Tell me what happened at work that made you want to move to Fiji.
Ask me questions that give me a reason to sigh before I speak.
We'll get together when the sun gets sleepy.
Firelight is enough illumination for our lazy conversations.
We can whisper secrets and yodel under a celestial disk.
We will add strands to the bonds that
weave us into a common cloth.
I have no desire to see and be seen,
Unless the ones I am with can recognize
when I would love an icy lemonade.
I have no frivolous moments
to sprinkle on the unworthy.
Come, sit beside me.
Let's sprawl by the glowing hearth and
Remember what makes us feel whole.

WAVES

The absence of my mom is a funny thing. I did not see her much during the past year, but the sound of her voice on a recording brought her presence back in full force.

Today, my siblings and I were going through tasks that needed to be handled. I was okay. When I am focused, I can keep my emotions in check.

Then, while driving in the car tonight, listening to stories about Mama brought her death back to center stage and I lost control. All the crying won't change what happened, but it does soothe my inner turmoil for a while.

I saw this photo and it made me think of all the times Mama was holding me steady and I could rest in her arms.

My Lola (grandma) is smiling so broadly. That makes me feel good because this was shortly after she lost my Lolo (grandpa). This picture reassures me that joy, contentment, peace, affection, and good times with family can soften grief.

Lola had lost her dearest love. She lived another 22 years, immigrated to a new continent, and built a life with her growing family in America. Imagine all the adjustments she had to make at the age of 75. She did not capsize or drown. She kept going forward.

I do not know how many more years I will have. That part is uncertain. I do know I can count on more holidays, milestones, celebrations, sorrows, and warm embraces in the times to come. I am absolutely sure of that.

In the meantime, I will ride the undulating emotions of grief, getting more accustomed to staying afloat with practice.

HOW'RE YA DOIN'?

My eyes are open, but what I see lurks in my memories. I'm not fully present. I may answer questions, but my words are generated automatically. Opinions, directions, thoughts, and reactions are coming from a robotic nervous system, which does not need much input from me.

Am I hungry? A little. Have I eaten recently? Perhaps. Thank you for offering to make a meal, pick up an order, or deliver extra groceries.

Twenty years ago, when my dad passed away, the week between his death and burial slipped by. I took care of arrangements, honored work obligations, and dealt with innumerable details. Am I able to recall specifics? Vaguely.

There is a similarity to that era now. When Mama left us, I slipped into a kind of half-awareness. Thank goodness for my attentive husband and loving circle.

Today, I did not push myself to be productive, check tasks off my to-do list, or change out of my pajamas before late afternoon. Demands felt too heavy.

It is International Dog Day, so I took note of how Riley and Raven handle life.

When they are drowsy, they collapse, as Raven did in front of the fireplace. If their stomachs growl, they munch on food in their bowls. If a noise or intruder distracts them, they switch focus immediately, but return to their naps if there is nothing urgent. If my hubby or I walk into a room, their tails wag in welcome, occasionally at a slow-motion pace.

They exist in the ever-present, the right-this-second, the eternal now.

I am getting the hang of that.

Most tasks can wait. Chores are done in order of greatest necessity. My only priorities are writing this daily post and caring for our grrrand-doggos.

This #2023bigyearproject gives me a reason to examine my emotions and frame them in a way that makes them clear to a reader. In a while, the most avid audience for these notes will be me. (Is that sentence grammatically correct?) There is every possibility that my mind will gloss over this period of mourning. I will need these daily entries to understand what I went through, how I handled calamities and delights, why I made decisions, and when the light broke through the fog.

During a text thread, our cousin Michael suggested a workshop leader would help my sister "pour painful energy into beautiful mourning." My sister quipped that a new song title could be "Oh What A Beautiful Mourning." I think I will borrow it to describe this season of life.

BUDDY SYSTEM

Who nudges you to be good to yourself? Who do you have on speed dial? (Is that still a thing?) Who would you pick up from the airport when their red-eye flight arrives? Who would lend you spare clothes when you are drenched from a storm?

Who will listen as you rant, cry, hoot, and holler over a story you have repeated too damn many times?

Hang on to those who fill these roles in your life. They may be relatives, chums, pets, or your favorite staff person at a local business. They are rare and valuable.

They are worthy of sharing a piece of delectable cake at midnight after you help them move to a third-floor walk-up apartment.

August 28, 2023

SURVIVORS

Many days after serving their initial duty, these stalwart roses continue to open their petals. I pulled them from their original bouquets and arrangements for this grouping of hardy players.

Nine days after Mama's funeral, we are also holding on day to day, drinking water, reaching toward sunlight, standing tall.

Over the past three weeks, I have seen, hugged, spoken to, and met many, many people who loved my mom and our family. We were surrounded by gentle arms as we took steps forward, and especially when we faltered. I never felt alone.

Slowly, I have reached out toward my out-of-state supportive circle. I have not been able to connect because of, well, stuff going on. Hearing the voices of my dear ones from afar has been restorative. I felt their energy even though they were not here. I was buoyed by their prayers, good wishes, and messages.

I believe positive energy finds its way to its recipient through distance, time, and silence. It is not deterred. It is unwavering.

It keeps us alive.

I understand biological laws. Humans need water and food to survive. I maintain that we also need companionship to thrive in this universe. We have to believe hands will catch us when we tumble. We must know that kindness waits for a chance to protect the vulnerable. We exist because we think we matter.

My parents were devoted to the four of us. They worked doggedly, through seemingly endless shifts, when they were depleted, and when they would have preferred to sleep just thirty minutes more. I am here because they never gave up on me, even when I was a royal pain.

I am grateful for their tenacity, sacrifice, sense of humor, and stubborn drive. I realize now that they taught us to be our best selves.

I wish I had told them so more often, but somehow, I believe they know we are their biggest fans.

FAR AND AWAY

Your essence is sighing in the wind, rippling in a brook, hiding behind clouds, illuminating leaves against a black sky, breathing through me, in me, with me.

Ollie Ollie oxen free. Come out, come out, wherever you are!

Beyond the veil. In another dimension. Up there. With the saints.

Not here. Not HERE. Not. Not.

Not.

No longer with me. No longer with us. Out of sight, always on our minds.

Still, not here.

I can conjure up your image, humming as you add a bit of this, a handful of that, enough sauce to darken the broth, and just a few drops of something to make the dish fragrant.

One measure of a song you sang makes me jump in at the refrain, alto line blending with the melody. The tune stays with me for hours, the soundtrack for that afternoon.

This is how it will be from now until I finish Earth School. I will bring back pieces of you, creating a talisman of sorts from memory.

The distance may be too far to breach in person, but I can instantly pull you to my side with a thought.

Hover nearby now and then, won't you?

August 29, 2023

EQUILIBRIUM

Yesterday, we took a short walk, arm in arm on a warm August evening. Today, I have been doing laundry for several hours. I had cold spinach pizza for lunch. My hubby made chicken fajitas for the first time. It was a delicious dinner.

We have done ordinary things on a regular weekday. It has been awesome!

This morning, I woke up after a full, uninterrupted, 7.5-hour sleep. Wow! I was alone in our house: first time to be by myself since Mama left us.

I checked social media, email, texts, and business threads. My cousin sent videos she took during the funeral service. As I watched them, I cried deep, heaving sobs. These tears have been waiting for the chance to be released.

Although I attended the service, I did not have the luxury of watching like a bystander. I was hyper-focused on what was happening, giving signals to stop and end parts of the program, standing to speak, and doing all sorts of tasks. I tried to be in the moment, but also needed to be a host.

Today, I was just a daughter who missed her mom.

That is why it felt so good to hang and fold clothes, chat with my best guy, make a few necessary phone calls, and tidy my home.

Life asks for our attention, effort, and concentration. It does not stop for grief.

I am thankful I can accomplish some vital chores while listening to favorite songs.

I am grateful for the kind souls who surround me.

I appreciate the compassionate Internal Revenue Service agent who said, "Before we begin, please let me offer my sincere condolences on your mother's passing. Moms are very important." I had spoken to at least three other agents who were all-business, efficient, and knowledgeable. They were helpful, but they did not offer the warmth and humanity that their colleague did.

One heartfelt phrase changed my entire experience. It transformed an hours-long ordeal into an act of love and devotion. Customer service matters, my friends. So do gentle hearts.

SUPER BLUE MOON

We could see the dark craters of Earth's satellite as we walked under a cloudless sky. Our shadows were sharply defined against the white sidewalk. The air had a crispness that felt bracing. I was more awake when we returned.

Today was momentous, Mama-ntous, Mom-entous. I had to submit paperwork with the County Clerk's Office.

I had to state my business at three places: the security checkpoint, the reception desk, and the clerk's window. "My mother passed away and I am here to file her will."

The receptionist gave genuine condolences and I almost wept.

Every time I say the words aloud, it's as though I must catch my breath first. It's a declaration of truth that my heart has not yet fully accepted.

I was grateful for my husband's steadying presence. Last night, I only slept about three hours. I had been anticipating today's errand and felt such an uneasiness. He drove while I watched scenery go by.

The clerk did her job quickly and well. All my anxiety had been groundless. It was a relief to collect my papers and walk away.

I stepped outside and took big gulps of fresh air. The sky beamed with bright August cheer. A slight breeze kept us comfortable.

Today was National Grief Awareness Day. That felt fitting.

As we walked under the cool light of a grand full moon, I could feel my mom's smile.

COVERING MY BACK

My dad had a tuxedo tailored for a concert. I nabbed the jacket for myself when he died.

It fit surprisingly well even though he was taller than I. I'm not sure if I could conduct a choir or symphony while wearing it, but I managed to fare well during both his funeral and my mom's. I needed to feel his determination and strength during those ordeals.

During the burial, I accidentally popped off the button holding the waist closed. I carefully put it in the coat pocket. One of the buttons on the right-hand cuff had fallen off more than twenty years ago, but could not be found. I hesitated to fix it because I liked the tiny flaw. After Mama's services, my husband brought the jacket to our favorite dry cleaner. He showed the errant waist button.

We got the dry cleaned and mended tux back today. To my astonishment, both buttons had been sewn back on! The marvelous tailors had replaced the missing cuff button. I hopped around with joy. The jacket feels whole once again.

Maybe this was symbolic of my parents reuniting. It felt like a reward for laying both of them to rest.

I hope I have an elegant place to wear this special piece of clothing one day soon.

I think it would make my folks happy to see me take it out for a celebration.

MESSAGE TO OUR LOVED ONES

Mama was our touchstone. She reminded us of who we are and where we came from. She watched over our family after Daddy passed away almost twenty years ago. Imagine being the sole parent for all that time, especially while missing your beloved desperately.

Before August began, Mama had gotten a diagnosis of cancer. At 91, she opted not to have chemotherapy or surgery. She felt that those extreme treatments might shorten her life. On August 4th, she began home hospice care. Angel's Grace Hospice is an amazing organization that provides hospital beds, oxygen tanks, and nursing care for no charge. Medicines were provided for a nominal fee.

She told us, "If there is a Hell, it is this terrible pain." That broke my heart. I knew she struggled to maintain a conversation because of her agony. She did her best to focus on our faces, give us her sweet smile, and sing along with my brother's music on ukulele and guitar. She loved to sing "Moon River" and "Tonight You Belong to Me." Her distinctive soprano voice was not as strong as before, but it was still clear.

In a few days, she had difficulty speaking and was in bed most of the time. She communicated, but her words were sometimes whispered and often had to be gestured. Ironic because she worked as an interpreter for years. Languages were her specialty. Suddenly, at the end of her life, she had to rely on body language and the understanding of those closest to her.

She had asked my brother to keep her illness a secret. A few days after hospice began, she relented and allowed us to let our circle know of her condition.

We called relatives and close friends. Several dear ones visited her at home. Mama was able to FaceTime or Zoom a few people. Those in the medical profession knew right away how fragile her situation was, how close she was to leaving us.

I asked for prayers from my social media crew. I needed to borrow the strength of others, had to have my faith bolstered. I was in denial for a few days. Unfortunately, there were precious few of them left.

My cousins Bonnie, Kathleen, and Geanie all practice the healing arts. They came to help, as did other dear ones. Mama was a nurse for decades. It was as though all the good care she had provided came back to her when she needed it.

On Monday, August 14th, I was awakened by a vision. It felt like a glimpse of the souls waiting for Mama's arrival. That was enough. I leaped out of bed and told my husband we had to go to my mom's place immediately.

We reached there about half an hour later. Mama was with us about 90 minutes more.

She still smiled a bit when I joked with her. She could no longer communicate well. She was weak. It was hard to watch her surrender to the pain.

Over the last two weeks, she changed from moaning random words of anguish to saying, "Thank you, Lord." My sister had spoken to her about seeing these trials as a way to show others her faith. She decided to embody gratitude instead of despair.

I had a few minutes alone with Mama on that final morning. I described my vision and told her that Daddy was waiting for her. Their 65th anniversary would be in two days. I said it would be wonderful if they could celebrate it together. After twenty years, she no longer had to be a good soldier. She had done enough. I assured her that we would all be okay. I asked for her forgiveness and told her I would only remember the love.

When she passed, my siblings and I were each holding her, speaking words of affection and assurance. We sobbed but kept speaking to her until her last breath.

My cousin phoned our nephew, a pastor in Dallas, Texas. He was able to pray with us. As he gave a benediction, we could see Mama letting go. She waited until he said Amen, then exhaled one breath more. That told us that she had heard every message we gave her until her eyes opened in Paradise.

We had some time with her before the funeral staff took her into their care. Bonnie, Kathleen, and Geanine, three of my cousins, were able to say goodbye in person. They have stood beside us through so much of Mama's life. My brother's good friend Linda was there. She had helped Mama a lot over the past two years. Steve held me up. These souls were with us at the end, too. I told my daughter Aubrey over the phone when her Amma was going. She was able to go home and see her husband Mike when I told her that Amma had gone to Heaven.

Many of our loved ones were able to visit her in hospice and attend her services. Linda and Wes set up video equipment so that others could watch the services from a distance.

During Mama's wake and funeral, we received hugs. Kisses, words of love, flowers, gifts, and financial help. It was astonishing to hear all the stories of how Mama had left a positive impact as a nurse, volunteer, choir member, neighbor, co-worker, aunt, great-aunt, sister, sister-in-law, and friend. These wonderful souls let us know that we were not alone.

My mom was the ultimate hostess. She liked nothing better than welcoming folks to her home, feeding them delicious food, and making them feel special. Our family chose to bury Mama in a bright red dress and a sparkly jacket that my dad had chosen for her. She looked elegant and ready for a grand celebration.

Although I feel her absence keenly, I keep imagining all the joyful reunions she is having. Her parents, grandparents, siblings, dear relatives, close friends, and pets must be running to her. That though has sustained me during these difficult days.

My siblings and I are so grateful to all of you who have expressed your beautiful wishes, prayed for and with us, given such generous presents, and joined the services for our Mama. You have warmed our aching hearts, given us reasons to laugh and smile, brought comfort, and followed up. We know how much you cared for mama and our family. We wish we could give every one of you a big hug and express our appreciation in person. The coming days, months, and years will be altered, but we know that Mama's presence will remain.

Thank you for all you have done to lighten our burden of grief.

Evangeline Altamero Tabayoyong
February 2, 1932 — August 14, 2023

JO-JO TABAYOYONG MURPHY

WADING THROUGH
FRESH MUD

SHINING PEBBLES ALONG THE PATH

When you are maneuvering through strange waters, do you appreciate big, clear, shiny markers that let you know you are going the right way? Are you grateful for anyone holding a lantern to illuminate shadowy sections?

In ancient times, we used paper maps to navigate on long car trips. Woe to those who had no co-pilot to shout out turns, exits, and rest stops before we drivers zipped past them. Sometimes we realized that our treasure maps were outdated, and locations had changed. We got turned around much too frequently. We had to develop instincts like Himalayan sherpas to understand directions to our desired destinations.

We argued a lot.

As my family makes our way after our matriarch's passing, I often wonder whether I am doing tasks well, catching all the proper details, and remembering a myriad of important steps. My notes fill a yellow legal pad. My mind swirls at bedtime.

All this is happening while my siblings and I grieve.

Today, I was making lots of phone calls, researching, asking questions, and learning surprising information. My patient, loving Cousin Annabelle and her dear husband gave me some valuable insights and history on an important matter. I met several kind souls as I went through my day.

My go-to florist buddy helped us send a birthday plant to my auntie. It was a treat to hear her enthusiastic voice on a wearying day.

I have found that people who have experienced a profound loss are the most sympathetic to others who are suffering. They know how overwhelming the pain can be. They become gentle guides through ominous tunnels and shine brightly.

My daughter went with us to handle some issues. As we left an office building, I noticed a white feather firmly affixed to the hood of our maroon car. It had not gently fallen from a clear blue sky. It had been glued by some weird substance to the center of that metal cover.

I believe that angels drop feathers when they are nearby. I took this distinct bit of fluff as a sign that Mama saw our efforts and cheered us on. (She must have made sure her signal would not blow away during our drive!)

As a reward after a busy week, my hubby and I drove to a Filipino market and bought some karioka dessert balls. They are made of sticky rice coated in a sweet caramel sauce. I devoured two sticks' worth.

The path may feel harrowing. Our legs may ache. We may feel lonely in a few sections. Let us keep walking forward.

At the worst times, I hope we can be light bearers for each other.

And let us remember to pat ourselves on the back. Let us reward ourselves for doing our best in difficult situations.

Let us remind ourselves that the smallest acts may have the greatest impact.

September 2, 2023

THROUGH

One more step forward. Rest if you must but keep moving.

This has been a long, wearying slog. Not gonna lie, some of the steps forward have been through thick, sticky, icky mud. (Not a fan of gooey!)

The best part of this week has been having my daughter and son-in-law back. They have helped me and my hubby take care of tedious, confusing details. My ability to organize is good. My daughter's is outstanding. I have been awed many times this week.

As an extra treat, we got to see our wriggly, joyful, cuddly, loving grrrand-pups for a bit.

After working on tasks for a few hours, we went our separate ways.

My darling, thoughtful fella made the rest of the day more holiday-like. We did a Costco run. (I loves me a browse through that place!) There were tasty samples, interesting new products, and lots of steps for my Fitbit tracker.

After a few more errands, we discovered we were near Gumii, a fantastic Korean restaurant. The bulgogi and mandu were savory and fresh. Our bellies were satisfied.

This evening, my hubby and I allowed ourselves the luxury of disappearing into our favorite video game. I fought epic battles, won fabulous rewards, and became more powerful. It was a great way to clear my swirling thoughts.

An old friend once heard about an ordeal I was facing. His advice still comes to mind when I am in the middle of dark expanses. "Sometimes the only way out is through."

This current road may be full of wild challenges. How fortunate I am to have ridiculously cool companions along the way.

SIGNS ALONG THE WAY

A strange cloud formation caught my attention as we drove along the expressway. It looked like the tracks a hopping bird's wet feet might make on a dry sidewalk.

I snapped several shots. The one I liked, (slightly enhanced to make the clouds more visible) seemed to show those bits of fluff following the line of electrical wires. I cannot take credit for framing the shot well. I give a hat tip to beautiful synchronicity.

As we walked down a street in Chinatown, my hubby asked me to take a photo of him with a senior citizen crossing sign. We had just been chatting with friends about our ages qualifying us to be considered silvers.

Nice to know we have a designated place to make our way across a busy road.

We received a spontaneous invitation to dinner with good friends. I'm so happy we went! It was a chance for a lighthearted mini reunion among folks who always lift our spirits.

After our meal, I had a luscious dessert at Mango Mango. It's a favorite spot, but its distance keeps us from going there more often. Ooh. Ahh.

Finally, we happened to be near the airport. My sister needed a ride and we were able to take her home. More synchronous pieces creating an elaborate picture.

We made small decisions, which led to other choices, which eventually led to my sister and brother staying over at our home tonight.

When you are presented with enticing options, pick the ones that make you giddy, eager, delighted, or just plain ready for excitement!

You may not see the whole path you have created when all you can see is one wet outline of a footprint. You just have to trust that hindsight will be able to show you the exquisite tapestry you have formed.

Remember, if tiny wisps are able to march across a vast September sky in a lovely pattern, there's a 100% certainty that you are meant to be right here, right now, reading my words.

Thank you!

LUCKY

Mama was the eternal optimist! One of her favorite sayings was, "when I win the lottery …." She took chances, grabbed opportunities, and thought something amazing could happen any day.

This photo was taken at Mama's birthday celebration that we held at a local casino. Mama and one of her best friends won big that night. All of us shared their excitement.

Looking back, I realize having her as my mother was one of my biggest strokes of good fortune.

Day 249   #2023bigyearproject

VISIBLE MEANS OF SUPPORT

A heart that has endured the pain of loss is more resilient. A heart that has been broken is stronger where it has mended. A heart that has felt profound agony recognizes that anguish in others' eyes.

These are a few of my cousins. Every one of us has lost at least one parent. Some have said goodbye to siblings, both parents, and in-laws.

That made their presence at Mama's services more poignant and meaningful.

They have wept at the side of their ailing mothers and fathers.

They have had sleepless nights, minds spinning with grief.

They have explained death to children and grandchildren.

We have prayed for each other.

We have been pallbearers at the funerals for our loved ones.

We have held each other up when we collapsed.

We have told great stories to remind us of hilarious experiences, mildly threaten us about youthful escapades, and strengthen our faith when we falter.

We represent many generations and branches of our family.

We have a cute family resemblance, right?

HOLDING TOGETHER

Good news can come in tiny packages. This evening, Covid tests for my husband and me came back negative. Thank God.

After a very emotional August, this was a hard first week of September. We are still grieving and working on tasks to tie up my mom's affairs. Having the possibility of illness dangling over our heads was, well, not a picnic.

I took the chance to rest after hearing we were exposed. I had two rare unscheduled days. What a gift! Even though I did not run around, doing, doing, and doing, necessities got done, done, and done. (Pssst, the world spins without my help!)

My husband cooked delicious meals and made sure I ate enough. (Sometimes, I neglect to refuel.)

I allowed myself to contemplate everything that had happened in the past month. I pondered, sought understanding, cried, smiled, and gave thanks. I allowed others to help me. (Probably the hardest thing I did.)

This evening, I joined a Bible study group led by family members. What a healing experience that was. Seeing their faces and hearing their voices on the Zoom call was so moving! They shared their insights, knowledge, grace, and kindness generously.

Jumping on the call was a spontaneous decision. Being on the call felt like divine intervention.

Over the past few weeks, a circle of loving hearts has surrounded all of us who knew and cared for my mom. When we were frail and struggling, gentle hands held us up, wiped away our tears, prayed for us, offered their strength, and applauded our efforts.

It has been extraordinary.

I have many thank you notes to write. This labor of love has been overdue. I did not want to rush it. I wish I could hug every soul who has been beside us, in person or from a distance.

Nothing I can put into a card would be able to convey how significantly every compassionate act has affected our family.

Thank you all for creating a soft, caring net around us that kept us from shattering.

STATUS

Metrics can show patterns. Data can track trends. Graphs and pie charts can translate numbers into visuals.

I take my blood pressure regularly, weigh myself consistently, and see doctors when necessary.

Today I realized I had not taken a selfie in a long time. That surprised me because I used to do that often during the Pandemic, when subjects for photos were limited to me and my Quentin Quarantino hubby.

Took a few today. Played with portrait mode on my phone's camera.

Can you tell I got 4-1/2 hours of sleep?

It's tricky to measure emotions. Trained psychologists and other mental health professionals are able to make assessments, but it's not like feelings can be assessed by an objective machine.

If I had to say, I would give myself a good score. My heart is healing. I'm not yet functioning at my most efficient level, but I am productive, cheerful, and sociable. I have an appetite, too. (Last night I had such a craving for pizza!)

Right now, that's enough.

September 9, 2023

ON THE UP AND UP

Once upon a Sunday, a cloud plume drew my eyes higher and higher. I used the panoramic feature on my phone to capture its height.

As my hubby will tell you, I am a big fan of the sky. While he drives, I frequently ask him to pull over. I might pause before getting in the car when we are parked. I often invite him to go outdoors to look at cosmic phenomena.

During airplane trips, if I get a window seat, cloud scenes fill my camera's memory banks.

I once read a book that described a fantasy bedroom where a young girl could pull back her ceiling and raise her bed so that she could watch the moon and stars. If I weren't so jittery about heights, that would be perfect for me!

My guy laughed when I said that I would request a specific job in Heaven. I would ask to be in charge of sunrise and sunset scenery.

Can you imagine the color palette, texture options, lighting effects, and weather I could use?

I applaud whoever has that responsibility now.

I'd be willing to share my job with others. After all, audience members would have excellent seats for every display.

THE RAIN FALLS ON EVERYONE

As I contacted our circle about my mother's passing, I caught up with the latest news from each person. I noticed one universal fact: every soul is dealing with something challenging. Earth School is hard.

One uncle needs eye surgery. Two aunts took tumbles and had to have x-rays. Another person was getting cardiac tests. Someone else was caring for a partner who was ill. My mom's contemporary was dealing with the confusion of dementia and had a tough time understanding the reason for my call.

No one is spared from having woes.

What I also learned was that attitude makes the biggest difference in how one deals with challenges. Those who see calamities as tests that may be conquered have an easier time. Those who can laugh at the absurdities enjoy the adventure. Those who interpret every ailment as a punishment seem to suffer more desperately. And those who look for the meaning behind the lessons are more serene.

Where do I fall in this gradient? I tend to be optimistic. I face each day with the belief that I can probably handle whatever befalls me. I have a great support system. My family is known for laughing at inappropriate times, so we end up making each other feel better by joking about issues. I remind myself that I have endured, survived, and outlasted many disasters.

I am not, however, a Pollyanna. I do not try to make light of terrible situations. One thing that mystifies me is well-meaning folks telling those who are suffering to "stop crying!"

Excuse me. If I have lost a loved one, gotten a frightening diagnosis, been fired, or lived through a fire/flood/robbery, I will bawl my eyes out, with or without your permission.

Public tears are not something I like to show. I'm more likely to wail in private. As I have been living through the past few weeks, I have allowed myself to weep any time emotions become too much. I finally have given myself permission to admit weakness, surrender to my feelings, and ask for help.

Whew! Took a lot of therapy, maturing, and harrowing experiences to get to this point.

Again, I repeat that I am not Pollyanna. I am not immune to despair. I have faced so many demons that I have named a few of them. Watch out for Fred! He's a beast who whispers mean judgments around 3 a.m.

My mourning has been public. I have a daily post on Facebook and Substack where I talk about anything I have noticed as I go through life. The topics can be anything from cleaning tips (very few) to sunsets (frequent) to the crushing grief I have felt during the past month. No filters. No censorship. No hiding.

That has been how I have released my mourning. When ideas are brought out into sunlight, they become less scary. When I ask for the advice of others who have been through these kinds of ordeals, I have learned some priceless concepts.

We are divine beings living a human experience. We may choose to address our circumstances as enlightened creatures or lowly beasts. The time we spend on Earth will be the same. Our mileage, and enjoyment of that time, will vary.

September 14, 2023

JO-JO TABAYOYONG MURPHY

STANDING BESIDE OTHERS

I HEAR YOU IN THE STILLNESS

There was a new emptiness, where there had once been significance.

A clear, strong voice was silent. She had been able to hold a rich, high note that pierced beyond the sounds of other singers in a crowded church. When she sang among strangers, I would giggle to myself in anticipation of the shock they would experience as she opened her mouth to redefine familiar hymns.

Mama was confident about her ability to sing with her rare soprano voice. I was proud of her, as were my other siblings. Daddy made sure she was a member of all his choirs. He knew she could anchor the women.

Eleven days before she left us, my brother strummed a ukulele and sang a sweet duet with her. I was charmed by the sight of their smiles as they crooned a piece they knew well.

Coincidentally, I had fallen in love with the same song a few months earlier. I have two versions of it in my phone's library.

I hummed it often during the next few weeks, especially when I missed my mom.

"Moon River" was another tune she sang for us. After she died, I have heard it during meaningful moments. We believe it's one of the ways she lets us know she is nearby.

The veil between heaven and earth is thin, I know Mama watches us with compassionate eyes. She wants to send comfort in a way that we understand. When words could not convey elusive feelings, we could reach each other with melodies, lyrics, and rhythms.

Mama has been with Jesus for six months. My hubby and I passed by her apartment the other day at sunset. I could see furniture and a large television through the patio door. I was glad that light and sound filled the spot where we had said our goodbyes.

I have not performed much since last August. I even asked to be spared from playing during Mama's services. Now that some time has gone by, I find myself longing to create sounds again.

Perhaps my cello's voice can convey the depth of my grief, the height of my gratitude, and the connection it will always give me to my parents. May its notes rise to heaven.

February 22, 2024
5:34 a.m.

ANTHONY

A while ago, this orchid was spectacular. As soon as it burst out of its pale bud, it reached for sunlight and turned its face upward. Perhaps it felt called and looked for whoever knew its name.

After its peak, it did not fall off the branch, as the other blooms had done. It kept a firm grip of the stalk, still pointed toward light. I applauded its tenacity and admired its artistry.

Who was I to say when it was time for it to release its hold?

This week, I finally snapped off the dedicated branch. Other orchid plants had grown and produced healthy, vibrant flowers. This plant had nothing new to offer. I thought some gentle pruning might encourage it to send out another green shoot.

This morning, I was shocked to hear of a young man's sudden passing. I have known him since he was a little guy. Anthony was quiet but had a shy smile that could melt a heart of stone. His parents are kind, warm, and generous. He gave them such joy and made them proud.

I could sense their profound loss, but I could not accept or understand it. I wished I had the power to give them strength, ease their pain, or bring him back to them. All I could do was hold a sweet memory of seeing him playing Nerf basketball in his cousin's bedroom. It comforted me to think of him laughing and wanting to be part of all the fun.

A few hours after this news, a friend let me know that our ex-co-worker's husband passed away in his sleep. He and I were almost the same age.

I reeled. He leaves another hole in a family that loved him dearly.

I was home most of the day while we had some work done by skilled tradesmen. I had plenty of time to think of the impact these two souls had upon those who treasured them. I lifted up prayers that these grieving people be given arms to hold them, warm-hearted folks to console them, and peace to envelop them so they could rest.

I thought of the stalwart orchid that hung on long past the time of its exuberance. I believe we hold on to the memories of our loved ones like this. Even though their spark of vitality is gone, we can keep the essence that made them beautiful, cherished, and significant. Their presence will always remain with us in some form.

I hope they were met in Paradise by those who knew and adored them when they were thriving on Earth.

ALL SAINTS DAY

Your light is remembered
In the flicker of a candle,
The warmth of a child's eyes,
The perennials planted so lovingly,
And the stories we tell each other around the fireplace.

I keep your keychain hanging near the back door.
I wish you could return from a quick errand.
We'd talk about the day you had
While sipping tea on the porch.

During a special service,
a bell is rung as the roll call is recited.
We have so many to honor this year.
I will murmur your name.

Along with the dignitaries, sports heroes, film stars, and artists,
You left us much too soon,
Though I have no magic number of years
I would have designated as
Your fair share.

If you may journey between realms
On this sacred day,
Visit my dreams, please.
Tell me an old, familiar joke.
Hum my favorite tune.

Give me a reason to wake up in a sweet mood.

This day is dedicated to you.
Most are.

October 31, 2020

ESCAPE

It is cold here.
My heart is weighed down with unshed tears,
anguish unexpressed,
and secrets that were shoved onto me.

In my mind, I can release myself from this prison.
I throw off dusty sandals and run through soft grass,
The wind blows all troubled thoughts behind me.

You may see my wrinkled brow and downcast eyes,
But you cannot stand beside me
 in the paradise of my imagination.

Some nights, my eyes will not close
And the moon gazes down
Without sympathy.

I look at darkened walls
All familiarity blurred
My senses catch the unseen.

I recite state capitals,
Irregular French verb tenses,
And last week's grocery list.

My energy is jolted
By those worries demanding
Contemplation.

When bright sun creates
Sharp, black shadows,
Contrast eliminates gradations.

Nuance, subtlety, blurred divisions
Make me waver
I know no certainties.

I know the anxious peering
Of a sailor who has lost his bearings
And must traverse strange waters.

Without fog horns blaring warnings
Or stars providing guidance,
My tiny boat drifts.

I lay down on a rocking surface
And pray that my surrender
Will bring me to a safe destination.

November 18, 2019

PROTECTIVE LAYER

I stepped on an upturned sewing needle once.
The sound of the puncture and my immediate scream
Reverberated through our silent home.
My husband and daughter ran to soothe me.

My skin is thicker where wounds have healed.
I learned to clear hazards more diligently.

I may tread more lightly,
I may shield myself from danger,
I might keep the ones I love in a protective circle,
But pain can creep past barriers.

I thought I was too wise to be vulnerable.
The warning signs seemed bright and unmistakable.
Do not ingest poisonous substances.
Mind the gap.
Slow down at this turn!

Where are the blaring horns
when a situation deceives me?
That relationship felt solid.
That person had kind eyes.
That bond shattered,
jagged edges piercing my shell.

How did I not see the traps?

I could keep a safe distance,
Shy away from entanglements,
or refuse to get involved.
Life would be calmer.

But solitary confinement is cruel.
I would not be Thoreau finding peace at Walden.
I would be a prisoner lying face down in a grey cell.
I would miss the warmth of a winter evening around the hearth,
Chattering about nothing and everything.

So, I remain open, trusting, and keen to be a friend.
I remain a citizen of a family nation.
I hold office hours for those who want to meet.

My skin acquires more scars,
And I do not cover them with mourning clothes.

August 1, 2019

RAINDROPS AND TEARS

Daffodils will gleam on our hilltop next Spring.
I promise to plant them for you.
I will let the hay get long and full,
Then I will gather it in thick bunches.
One will go to the stable next door.
The others will be shared with your buddies.

Tomorrow, I will take your ashes out in the moonlight.
As I scatter them, I will hum your favorite melody,
I will remember the ride we took on your last birthday.
I will sit and let a sugar cube melt on my tongue.
I will watch fireflies add their tiny stars to the field.

We were partners, you know.
We were meant to stay together a few more years.
I was not supposed to be alone,
Without you, the world feels unfamiliar.
I have no place to go that feels welcoming,

Was it selfish of me to beg you to stay?
Did you hear me wail when you closed your eyes?
Has your spirit kept me company this week?
May I join you soon?
Do you miss me, too?

As I stood in the barn yesterday?
I could have sworn I heard you.
As I ate a solitary dinner,
I could not taste anything,
but I am sure I saw you walking past my window.

We had a connection that will not be severed.
You may flee to another reality, planet, or universe.
My heart will cling to yours forever.
If I need your presence,
listen to my summons.

We can be together in my dreams.
We can still ride, comfort each other,
and feel that loving bond this way.
I will look for you as soon as I drift away.
Be there, please.

A year from now, the hill will gleam with yellow blooms.
Five years from now, our son will run to my arms.
Twenty years from now, he may bring a mate home.
Fifty years from now, I will still hold your memory dear.
Watch over us. Walk beside me. Wait for me.

June 26, 2021

SCAR TISSUE

A finger is permanently bent.
A lip pulls back in a severe angle.
One eye struggles to interpret light.
An illness deep inside ravages her spark.
This woman has known anguish.

A beloved husband was taken too soon.
A massive clot halted his life.
One minute he was speaking to his son,
Asking about a scouting event.
The next instant, he felt the shock of pain.

She has known tragedy.
She has witnessed the atrocities of a cruel war.
She makes the most of any resources at hand.
Increasing numbers of candles on her birthday cake
Mark the years she has filled with vivid memories.

Another might have buckled from the weight of her burdens.
Someone else might have cursed misfortune.
A weaker spirit might devote dwindling strength to whining.
This stalwart woman of faith keeps ministering to others.
Her hospice room becomes a sanctuary, a place for sacred work.

She is the matriarch of a growing tribe.
Grandchildren and great-grands have pet names for her.
She greets each one by name and with a glorious smile.
If asked, every descendant claims to be her favorite.
They believe this declaration wholeheartedly.

LOVE IN THE PANCAKE BATTER

I am not a healer.
My strengths lean toward artistic, creative ventures.
I do not know how to interpret graphs, vital statistics,
Scribbled prognosis notes, or beeping machines.
Words are my talismans and street signs.

So, I ask her to tell me stories of her life.
One day she recounts the births of her many children.
I hear details of birth weights and difficult labor ordeals.
This daughter was robust, this son arrived at lunch time.
She holds almost a century of history in her brain.

She speaks in soft, matter-of-fact tones.
I hear about seeing mothers' babies ripped from their wombs
And watching those infants speared by swords.
Maps would announce areas zoned for destruction.
Their citizens knew they would be gunned down.

She describes torture, scarcity, and fear
That came with an international war.
Yet, her tone never becomes disrespectful,
Her voice is just above a whisper.
We listeners feel our knees tremble.
Anger and despair grip our hearts.

But she also remembers acts of love:
Soldiers that spared her father's life
Because he cried out, "Christo Christo!"
A general who saw his young daughter in the eyes of her little sister.

She could recognize commonalities and forgive their failings.
After all this, she dispenses grace with a generous hand.
People have been led

To the God she serves.
They saw the way believing enhanced her life
And that was enough to bring them to the altar.

She leaves no room in her heart for bitterness or regret.
Her faith is unbreakable.
Her kindness is legendary.
Her beliefs spark a seed in every life.
Her scars are pliable, healing with softness.

June 7, 2019

HAVE YOU EATEN?

I was the breadbasket, the provider of sustenance.
My table always had an extra chair, plate, and welcoming smile for
anyone who was hungry.

I expressed my love through the delicious meals
that I prepared with delight.
My laughter and enthusiasm seasoned each tasty morsel, satisfying
needs that may not have been spoken aloud.

My intention was to fill others' emptiness
with warmth, comfort, ease, and peace.

Some called me a chef as I hosted feasts.
I thought of myself as a steward of goodness,
who distributed blessings that were given to me.

Remember me when you lift a spoonful of fragrant, savory broth.
Think of my smile when you taste an enticing new flavor.
Share your table with others who are crying out for succor.
These simple gestures will keep my passionate legacy vibrant.

In memory of Padma's brother
September 27, 2023

THE GIFTS WE BRING

Some of us are diplomatic. We are sensitive to others' feelings and calm wounds.

Some of us are detail oriented. We manage logistics, arrange deliveries, and provide information to a host of people.

Some of us are designers. We take raw materials and form them into exquisite art pieces.

Some of us feed hungry masses. We show up to an event with platters, trays, and baskets of delicious food.

Some of us handle technical issues. We manage equipment, balance light and sound, and provide expertise.

Some of us are musicians. We move hearts with familiar songs and evoke memories.

Some of us are practical. We anticipate needs, plan, and handle surprise situations with grace.

I am in awe at the collection of talented, generous, thoughtful folks who are moving Heaven and Earth to honor my late cousin. There are a thousand individual parts that must work in tandem so that his funeral will be meaningful, welcoming, comforting, and respectful.

Manong Samie, I hope you realize how much you were loved. May you watch our efforts over the next couple of days and feel at peace.

January 13, 2024

ASKING, ANSWERS

I asked to make an impact.
I was given a microphone.
I spoke my truth, whether or not I received a response.

I hoped to save the world.
I was given one spouse, one child, and two hands.
I faced my responsibilities and did my best, whether or not I felt effective.

I wished for peace.
I was given conflicts, disagreements, and differences of opinion.
I listened, shifted position when I learned more, and held my ground when
necessary.

I wept for the sick, the hungry, the homeless, the misunderstood.
I was given resources.
I shared, I offered comfort, and I prayed with them.

I prayed because I felt weak.
I prayed because the world seemed to suffer.
I prayed and saw that others also lifted their supplications toward the sky.

We stood up to make a difference,
One hand at a time,

One intention at a time,
One breath at a time.

I could sleep because I knew my prayers had been heard.

December 27, 2023

OUR VILLAGE

Tossing us back to the time we visited our friend Eden. She was in the last stages of the illness that took her from us long before we were ready to let her go.

That sunny light bearer is her daughter Niki. She was about the same age in this photo as her mom was when she and I met.

Eden and her brother Earl lived in Indiana, but they drove with their parents all the way to our church in Chicago every Sunday. The six kids in our two families grew up together, keeping in touch through school, marriages, kids, and all the experiences that life brought.

When we heard that Eden was fading, my sister, brother, daughter, and I took a road trip with May, her cousin. We went to help in any way possible and spend time with Eden and her two little girls.

I remember doing lots of laundry. I washed everything I could find, folded towering stacks of towels, and talked with our friend whenever she was awake.

This was one of my first times to witness one of my peers reach the end.

Eden was practical. We sorted her pajamas, and she decided which ones to donate, saying, "Well, I will never wear these again."

My heart clenched at those words. How unfair it was that a person who lived every second of her life with zest had to have such a short turn! Her daughters needed their mom. Her brother needed his sister. Her parents needed their daughter. We needed our friend.

One sweet memory was watching her kiddos run around the house and play. Eden had some fruit in a bowl. She fed it to her girls, singing out, "Do you love me? Then have a bite!"

Niki would stop by the table to open her mouth like a little bird in a nest. After eating a cube of sliced goodness, she leaned against her mom for a minute, then returned to play. There was so much affection between them. I can still see that scene as if it's on a movie reel of poignant moments.

We had to leave after a few days, but May stayed. Other relatives joined them. We returned when we heard Eden had gone.

Since then, we have had the joy of watching her girls mature into independent, bright, loving women who kept the wit, faith, and energy their mom gave them.

We have been part of the community for these young women, as our parents were for all of us. May this generation continue to nurture the next one with as much care and enthusiasm.

May we understand that each one of us matters.

BLEACHER SEAT

Tossing us back to my Auntie Tomasa's wake. I was asked to play for the service in Dallas. Since we had to drive to Texas, my niece Sarah generously offered her instrument so that I did not have to take my cello along.

My vantage point during such events is usually a chair positioned near the podium or somewhere else near the front of the room. I am placed among the floral arrangements, picture collages, and occasionally beside the casket or urn. I face the seated guests so that I can catch all the cues from officiants who are directing the proceedings. It has occurred to me that my view would be the same as that of the person being honored if they could witness it.

The survivors may be overcome by grief, not able to select meaningful songs or readings. In those cases, I either make suggestions or create a playlist of music that is meant to soothe, uplift, and comfort those who gather.

The person who has passed may have had favorite tunes that had a lot of significance. One of my church friends loved the musical *Les Misérables*. I kidded her that I would play "Master of the House" during her funeral. She laughed and thought that would be great! Alas, I was not able to participate in her celebration of life.

Fortunately, she did ask me to be the cellist for her husband's funeral. Among the familiar Methodist hymns, she told me there was one song I had to include. I agreed.

There were many emotional tributes from their children, dear friends, military cohorts, and community leaders. Through the course of the morning, I interjected music as the pastor requested. As the final rituals were being done and the Benediction was recited, I panicked a bit. No one had asked me to play his song yet. I had one last chance.

As the casket was prepared to be wheeled to the hearse, I launched into "Take Me Out to the Ballgame."

Grant, an avid Cubs fan, must have gotten a kick out of that timing! Eadie told me later that folks laughed about that for a long time.

LOVE NOTES

We drove to the cemetery in a long line of cars, hazard lights blinking, bright orange FUNERAL sign hanging on our rear-view mirror, iPod set to Shuffle. It was a somber ride because we knew we were saying goodbye.

As our wheels rolled to a stop, "When You Wish Upon a Star" began playing. My hubby and I spun toward each other as we recognized the song.

I played it at Jay's wake and funeral on Thursday and Friday. He was a fervent Disney fan. His sisters felt it would be a great tribute.

I marveled that Jay would send us this special sign as we arrived at Uncle Romy's graveside service.

I believe Jay was letting us know he would be welcoming Uncle Romy to Heaven.

Wow!

I texted a quick note to Jay's sisters and later told Uncle Romy's daughter what had happened. I also shared the message with our friend Ali. I wanted them to know that we had gotten this personalized sign.

There was no mistaking this because of its exquisite timing. Thank you, Jay!

Uncle Romy, I hope Jay and a host of other beloved souls cheered as you arrived!

***

As we reach the close of 2023, I have been meditating on what I have experienced, what lessons I have learned, and how I have changed. The questions are simple. The responses can be profound.

Key people have left, among them Mama and many other parents in our community. Four souls have gone since December 17th. There have been many, many days when it took a wrench, crane, and forklift to get me out of bed and back into the world.

To balance these losses, many sweet babies have chosen to join us over the past twelve months. The faces of their families glow with outrageous joy. Our ranks have been bolstered by these darlings. They bring hope, light, and reasons to knit baby blankets.

My honey and I have awakened in new places, tried unfamiliar flavors, and met amazing strangers who became friends. We have stood in awe at magnificent sights, gaped at artistic expressions that must have been wrought by angels, and taken thousands of photos. I gulped and crossed a bridge that swayed hundreds of feet above a chasm while I held my brave spouse's arm. I had a meeting with an Internal Revenue Service agent and spoke confidently. I reunited with dear ones from different parts of the country.

I learned that I can feel wretched, terrified, bereft, and exhausted, but continue to endure.

I learned that it does not take much to be wildly optimistic, jubilant, or content.

I learned to trust my abilities, intuition, and skills.

I learned to accept my limitations and forgive my imperfections. (That is not easy for a perfectionist, eldest daughter of immigrants!)

I learned that I may be separated by distance or opinion from the ones I care about, but our bonds will remain intact.

I learned that I would have what I need when I need it.

How have I changed? Superficially, I had fourteen inches of hair snipped off.

As a metaphor, it represented how I let go of belongings, activities, and ideas that no longer serve me well. I sought help to maintain my mental health. I began to grant myself as much grace as I offer others.

I know I am not the same person I was when this year began. I put a lot of effort into growing.

The word I focused on this year was Influence. I considered how I use my writing, where I devote my time and resources, and what I do when I interact with others.

How did I start ripple effects?

I am grateful to all of you who have read my posts, looked at the images I have shared, and responded in any way. Your energy has shown me that what I do matters. You have reminded me that I have a choice on the kind of impact I make.

You matter. You have influence. You create ripples.

May 2024 bring out the best in all of us.

JO-JO TABAYOYONG MURPHY

COMFORT AND JOY

OUTLINE

There was a bright, warm glow that afternoon, so long ago.

We had a picnic, played games on the grass, and watched the sun fall below the tree line.

I noticed your silhouette against our yellow blanket. The line of your cheek smooth and firm, your ponytail tousled by the breeze. I thought, for the thousandth time, that you were the most beautiful mother.

Your features were more familiar than my own. My oldest memories included your smile, the soft look in your eyes when you were proud of me, and the set of your jaw when you faced a difficult situation.

The thought of that ordinary spring outing comforts me still. I could draw your outline with simple, graceful lines.

You cast a shadow by standing against the setting sun. I wish I had taken a quick photo, but my recollection is as sharp and clear as a printed picture.

Perhaps I still see that figure whenever my sadness hides the light. I sense your absence and it creates a shadowy hole in my world.

I will allow the darkness to dwell with me for a while, seeing your absence in its familiar shape, form, and substance. It might be easier if I recognize your shadow as a sign that you are still nearby in some way.

Without the light, there would be no shadow. If I had not loved you, there would be no sorrow.

April 13, 2024

BUTTERFLIES DON'T STING

I saw a story about a family that raised caterpillars during the Pandemic. Their little boy loved watching them grow, form chrysalises, and become Monarch butterflies. As they pondered their next project, they wondered whether beekeeping would be a good hobby. The dad noted that the main difference is that butterflies don't sting.

We once visited a butterfly pavilion in a botanical garden. I was enthralled by the exquisite varieties that lived in this sanctuary. The deep blue wings of one breed astonished me. They seemed like imaginary creatures that had sprung from another realm.

Fourteen years ago, I saw a notice about an author who was visiting our local library. She was going to talk about writing books. On a whim, I signed up for the event. As sometimes happens, I squeezed too many activities into my day. That made me arrive a bit late at the meeting room. I sheepishly found a seat and tried to be quiet because the presentation had already begun. I had missed the introductory remarks.

As the woman gave suggestions and taught writing techniques, I finally realized that she was doing this in a room full of aspiring authors.

What?

I had not considered sharing any of my written thoughts with anyone other than my kind husband. Everyone in this group decided to attend the next meeting with a finished piece, limit 1,000 words. I was dumbfounded. I did not have a secret cache of poems, short stories, novellas, or postcards.

Though I loved reading, I had no dreams of becoming an author. Now and then I had created something that gained me a few compliments. Those plaudits had boosted my spirits temporarily, then I had gone on to the next thing on my ever-growing to-do list.

A friend of mine had organized this group. She encouraged me to return. I was too embarrassed to tell her that I had misunderstood the reason for the gathering. So, I sat at my computer and typed up a short essay about an encounter I had had with my little brother when we were kids.

To my surprise, I got a lot of positive feedback from the crew. That was enough to help me keep going. Twice a month, I would put my thoughts together and share my work with this bunch of strangers, who eventually became friends.

I believe we are led to ways we may use our innate gifts. Some may be able to whip up a nourishing meal from spiderwebs and dust. Others may heal with a gentle touch. I discovered that I like to wrangle phrases and touch hearts with my ideas.

If I had not decided to rush to that first meeting, despite being tardy, I would not have met this fate. Because I mustered my courage to read my initial story aloud, I discovered I had a unique way of expressing myself.

Since I began collecting memories I have self-published four autobiographies, one collection of fictional short stories and poems, and a workbook for children. Once I got past the self-imposed obstacles, I discovered an outlet for my emotions. Now I support others who may have hidden seeds that could bloom into spectacular flora. I try to shelter other caterpillars who have the capacity to become magnificent blue butterflies.

EVERY, EVERY, EVERY DAY UNTIL FOREVER

Step 1: Open eyes
Notice daylight
Take a breath
Acknowledge existence.

Step 2: Listen to birdsong
Notice wind rattling windows
Stretch limbs
Acknowledge persistence.

Step 3: Sniff crackling air
Notice rain
Set daily intention
Acknowledge responsibility.

Step 4: Appreciate warm bed
Notice soft slippers
Select clothes
Acknowledge vulnerability.

Step 5: Sip pineapple-orange juice
Notice bacon's crispness
Pack muffin
Acknowledge sustenance.

Step 6: Breathe in and exhale slowly

Notice heartbeat
Relish contentment.

Step 7: Close eyes
Notice fatigue
Pray for renewal
Acknowledge endurance.

Survived one more.

DECORATING MY CORNER OF THE SKY

Ordinary, mediocre, average, vanilla
Are not acceptable traits when one has been raised to be exceptional.
Expectations are high, goals were set at birth.
The pace has been punishing,

The criticisms have been blunt – and often self-inflicted.
Is there such a thing as enough?
I raised my daughter to believe that doing her best was perfectly fine.
How much more could I expect or demand from her abilities than that?

She still gave herself incredible targets and her aim has been true.
At this point, she has exceeded anything I have achieved,
Except that I managed to give birth to an incredible child.
I will take some credit for that, sharing it with my spouse.

I read biographies of leaders and dared to glimpse their lofty heights.
My aspirations were not modest at all.
My sixtieth birthday looms.
I take a furtive look behind me.

What do my footprints show?
Has this life been used to its best advantage?
The measurements for success are plentiful:
Bank accounts, degrees, property, influence.

If the scale I use to weigh my days is more forgiving
I might include the times I have brought comfort and joy to others.
With that assessment style in mind, I can count more points.
The list takes on an immeasurable quality.

My four-year-old Vacation Bible School student eventually released his mom's hand.
I applauded during beginners' recitals,
Surprised a depressed guy with cookies one morning,
Played music that made a little girl release her grief.

I fought back a bully who snarled at a harmless soul.
Questioned a ridiculous rule and brought about needed change.
Painted my neighbor's dresser for her son's room.
Sewed an elegant dress for an Irish doll that a customer had kept since childhood.

As resumes go, my bullet points don't show much status or any powerful roles,
Social media followers are a small, elite bunch.
Google does not bring up many postings of accolades or notorious deeds.
Have I made gold out of straw or have I left the wisps to dry in the sun?

REMNANTS

I may not be available tomorrow.

After all, who can predict what may occur?

In that case, the packages I meant to mail for birthday, graduation, congratulations, and good health will sit in anonymous piles. The good wishes were well-intentioned, but their impact will be lost.

Spider webs, tufts of fur, grey dust, and bits of paper will remain in the corners, edges, and parts of my floor that are covered by furniture.

"Tsk, tsk, tsk," some may say. "Housekeeping was not her forte."

From wherever I may dwell, I will have to agree. Making dark corners of my home unspeckled was not a priority. There was always a story to write, a dance of joy to shimmy, and a beloved to kiss with great abandon. That nudged away time for the vacuum to be wrestled out of hiding. That kept my hands so busy that I could not pick up a microfiber cloth. That made my days much, much more sparkly and memorable.

If I no longer have a functioning human form, the hundreds of unread email messages will be deleted. There should be no unseen text messages unless they were sent after my departure. I try to stay on top of at least one form of communication! All social media posts will revert to the one designated as my heir. I apologize in advance for any inconvenience. Others may be flummoxed by the years of comments, images, and nonsense that I have strewn onto the worldwide web. So be it. I enjoyed connecting through cyberspace with souls all over the globe.

I pray no one feels guilty that we did not chat more, exchange affectionate words, or spend hours doing wondrous activities. I want to know that there were enough chances for us to interact with sincerity, laugh without filtering

144

our snorts or howls, and give lingering hugs. Let us do what we can now and then go on without regrets.

Someone else will have to sort, wash, fold, hang, and put away laundry. I hope my dirty things will be cleaned one last time before being donated or recycled.

What will happen to the stacks of books on shelves groaning from their weight? I hope that I will eternally have access to all the knowledge and insights that were contained in those volumes, on my DVR to-be-watched list, and in newsletters that were carefully curated.

Will there be a palpable absence, or will the waters close over my head and obliterate all traces of my existence?

I have no idea what will become of my footprints, but I hope that somewhere a faint glimmer will indicate where I have made another being glow a little bit brighter.

EMERGENCY PROTOCOLS

In case of emergency, break out these techniques.

In case of embarrassment, remember that other people are not paying that much attention to you.

In case of failure, stop beating yourself up. Learn some lessons and move on.

In case of loss, sit still, think of a time when you enjoyed that person's presence. Recall details, touch mementoes, look at a photo.

In case of guilt, be gentle. You did not come into this world to inflict pain.

In case of anger, switch places with the antagonist. You have cut off people in traffic. You have been thoughtless. You have forgotten appointments. Next time, you may hope for someone else's forbearance.

In case of greed, take a moment to describe your most precious possessions. Chances are, they are not material goods.

In case of betrayal, understand that trust may be misplaced, but that you made yourself vulnerable for a reason. At one time, that person earned your respect. Next time, be careful, but realize that you are giving your heart to someone as human and flawed as yourself.

In case of joy, dive deeply into the exuberance of that moment.

In case of gratitude, express your appreciation loudly.

In case of unexpected gifts, remember that the next time you have the power to light up someone's day.

In case of success, be humble, but acknowledge the discipline, consistency, and persistence it took to gain it.

In case of amusement, laugh your damn head off. It's worth surrendering to glee.

In case of love, offer your loyalty, affection, and strength.

NEXT STEPS

As soon as I could put sounds together,
I began to make requests,
Demand that situations go my way,
Plead for cool stuff,
And ask for changes.

Shakespeare's witches stirred stew in a cauldron
And recited a spell.
Hogwarts students attended classes and wielded individualized wands.
Pastors held their hands on my head, spokespeople for the Christian God.
My Hindu friends chant on my behalf.
The atheists in my circle send research articles.

Eenie, Miney, and Mo guide my decisions.
The Magic 8 Ball has been known to venture an opinion.
The evening star has winked at me.
Wishbones, daisy petals, coins, and Tarot cards have also weighed in on
occasion.
In the end, I make the choices and deal with the aftermath.

Does divinity give a casual thought about what happens to these random
collections of cells?
Do we have any power/influence/sway over the events that affect us?
Are there any miracles assigned to me?

I learned prayers from adults in my world.
Their faith could be vehement, unshakable, and inspirational.
Then, my younger cousin declared she had stopped praying because God did
not give her the ability to fly.

Wait a minute!
I thought we could ask, and it would be given.
Were our petitions sorted, judged for merit, and ranked?!
Was I wasting my breath?

Her disappointment made me disillusioned for a time.
I knew that we should not bother God with pettiness,
but, who could say which prayers mattered?
I had heard that a tiny mustard seed could shift a mountain.

Today I stand at my mother's hospital bedside.
The scene is familiar.
We did this as my father took his final breath.
The people who waited with us loved him.
We sang hymns, closed our eyes, bowed our heads, and wept.

None of our actions kept him alive,
But I had hoped for him to be spared from further pain.
I believe my wish was granted.
As much as I loved Daddy,
I would not have forced him to endure one more second of pain.

If I were a shaman, I would know what to do in this situation.
If I were a witch, a preacher, a faith healer, or a magician,

I would have a plan of action.

I am none of those things.
I am a daughter who must surrender.
I am a human being who has limitations.
I am helpless, but not distraught.

There is a freedom in knowing that I must simply float down this river.
There is a release in understanding that my desires might be acknowledged
by a deity who reclines above the clouds,
but that those possibilities may not occur.

Instead, I ask for peace.
I want to be able to accept whatever happens.
I visualize a time when I can walk this path with serenity.

I just want to stop feeling anxious.
My imagination is one of my most powerful abilities.
I could create a new universe in one sunny afternoon,
complete with soundtrack, posters, and costumes.

Right now, I redirect my creativity toward
Seeing a time when my mom is either whole or at rest.

FLEETING

Rain became ice became snow
Became mud became puddles
Became a wet footprint on my porch
That faded in the afternoon sun.

As quickly as that,
Infant became toddler became teen
Became questioner became seeker
Became independent adult.

Though I took snapshots,
Wrote memoirs,
And recounted favorite tales,
One day melded into the next,
Rearranged the furniture and switched the clothes in my wardrobe.

I'll look more closely at this morning's routine,
Dismiss the tsk tsk tsk of my calendar,
And pay attention to the chatter as my household welcomes the morning.

I may not be able to catch a memory
In the palm of my hands,
But I can give a silent message of gratitude
When I notice the effervescent song of contentment.

PRAYER BEADS

Begin the litany and caress the first bead.
Be gentle.
The words must be said with sincerity,
Do not advance to the next orb
Until the prayer has been chanted completely,
Fervently,
Honestly,
And flawlessly.

This chain has been held by three generations of my maternal line.
The women have asked for healthy babies,
Faithful partners,
Abundant crops,
Successful business ventures,
And benign tumors.

One of my aunts broke the thick strand that kept
The beads together.
She had clutched it too tightly
When the telegram arrived.
Hours on her knees,
Begging,
Crying,
And surrendering
Had not gotten her petitions to the right gods.

Her daughter collected the strays
And restrung the array.
Once her mother's convictions faltered,

She handed over the beads without a word.
For her, they had lost their luster.
From then on, her lips never uttered another
Memorized phrase.

I was twelve when they came to me.
I had struggled so much to learn
The incantations that year.
I gave up Sunday afternoon bike rides,
Tuesday night ice cream breaks,
And the company of chattering students
Who thought life would give them everything they desired.

I had been fooled by empty promises,
Paper thin barriers,
And the ideas of forever, always, and never.
The day after my parents were dropped into
A rectangular plot,
Together for eternity,
My grandmother had gifted the precious beads to me.

I was the only possible recipient.
My siblings did not care for such archaic baubles.
They were anarchists, atheists, scientists,
And realists.
I was the one who dreamed.
The rest of my generation had been
Burnished by hardship until they shone.
My edges had not yet been smoothed.
When I felt the now-familiar weight of
The thirty-six charmed stones,
I felt as though the spirits of all my ancestors

153

Wept with relief.
An appropriate heir had been groomed.
I would carry on the traditions and
Perhaps,
The practice of repetitive, rhythmic,
Whispered, heartfelt requests
Would continue for another century or more.

Tonight I sat in front of an open door,
Feet dangling over the porch balcony.
The wooden counters moved forward in my hands
As I released the sentences over the garden.
Did I imagine the hush that silenced
Cardinals, cicadas, alley cats, and motor cars?
Lately, I stumbled between beads 28 and 29.
By the time I got to that point,
My resolve would falter.
I asked whether I needed to plod on until the last bit.
Could I simply recite ten verses and relax?
Wasn't a third of the dose enough to heal?
Didn't the listeners already understand what I needed?
How many hours had I spent
moving each bead
Along?

Have I redirected fate?
Has my will modified any outcomes?
Did my gratitude soften the heart of a deity?
Will anything get better because I asked?
Do these practices matter?
Do I?

My body knows the drill.
It's as though my feet could be pointed toward the East
And I would greet the sunrise like a dear friend.
Am I a conductor whose baton guides the performers?
Or am I a lackey who sweeps unending dust into a bin?

After half an hour,
The steady beat of well-rehearsed lines
Soothes my anxieties,
Assuages my fears,
Bolsters my strength,
And reaffirms my faith.

Pavlov's dog was taught to salivate on cue.
Mice maneuver complex mazes by sniffing out rewards.
Decades of doing my duty have molded my being.
Now, I end my ritual as I have countless other times.
I sigh,
Place my prayer beads carefully into the soft drawstring bag,
And stand.
I raise my arms upward
And stretch my fingers wide
Trying to catch all the blessings that are being directed
Toward my covered, upturned, expectant face.

THE SMALLEST DETAIL

I slouch on the love seat,
Looking out at our sunny front garden.
The troubles that perturb me
Feel cumbersome.
How will I bear their weight?

An earwig navigates folds of a bed sheet that covers the settee,
Protecting it from our rambunctious pup.
The bug's challenge is simply to move
From exposure to hiding
Without catching my eye.
Too preoccupied to halt its progress,
I let it slink away.

A housefly has been buzzing from room to room
For the past three days.
It just wants to return to the freedom of endless space.
The clues of light and air movement have deceived its senses.
Last night, it mistook the Australian countryside on television
For the mundane wilds of my hometown.
The hapless creature walked the perimeter of the glowing screen
And eventually was disappointed that the megapixels
Created an illusion.
This morning, my husband used the swatter
To send said fly to be with Jesus.

I admire the dogged march of ants and unwavering flights of honeybees.
They know their assignments,
Have their duties,
And serve their queens.
I have no such monarch to direct my movements.
Many hours are wasted on flailing about.

Are the scouts who leave their nests
Made of sterner stuff?
Are they elected by the hive brain
To seek food, face danger, and wander
Until their goals are met?
They bravely lay a trail for others,
Leaving a legacy of clues and the promise of reward at the end of a trail.

Not a bad life's work for a mite!

Do insects worship an omniscient presence?
Or are they born into their roles,
Serving without rebellion or resentment,
Forever and ever, amen?

I look for signs, messages from a benevolent universe,
That will show me how to solve my difficulties.
The gods send me these little Buddhas,
Reassurances that I am strong enough
To hoist my unwieldy, awkward burdens
And move forward.

ALCHEMY

Grasp both my hands,
Keep my gaze transfixed,
Assure me that what I am experiencing
Is guidance and not
A random infliction of pain.

Croon a familiar lullaby.
Recite phrases that were crafted
to save us from the shadows.
Tuck a talisman into my pocket
Or stand at the stove and cook spicy soup.

Brush my hair in front of an open kitchen window,
Use the weekly business report to fan away mosquitoes,
Direct our water hose along the hydrangea path,
Replace the top button on my winter coat.

Recognize worry in the line between my brows.
Rest a hand on my shoulder and
sense my trepidation.
Spot the tilt of my head from across a room
and walk over with a glass of lemonade.

We have collected the remedies.
The cure for despair has been inherited,
a gift passed from a grandmother to her noisy brood.
It rests deep in our cells and waits
for the moments when we sob or surrender.

We heal with a cooling balm.
We provide a bench for the weary.
We respond to the melody of an ice cream truck.
We skip as we move forward.
We know what to do.

IN THE ABSENCE

I hurt, so I ask the pain to speak, scream if it has to, but utter something I can hear. Otherwise, this ache swallows me whole with its silence.

During the long hours between moon and sun, I have lain in a quiet bed and waited for a sign. Do you exist on a plane where you can watch over me? Is my existence visible in that universe? Do you, maybe, not recall your previous existence?

Crying does nothing to bring you back.

Wailing does nothing but scare the birds and frogs outside my shuttered window.

I have seen too many sunrises through hooded eyes.

I need a new way of living from witching hour to sunup. Sleep declines to visit.

And so, I tally the number of times you made me laugh with unrestrained snorts, the rides we shared on strange new roads, the daily questions about whether I should eat a snack after 10 pm, and the notes you left as loving surprises on the kitchen counter.

As I count these gifts of grace, I sense your presence nearby. A scent, a breeze, a spark of light, the song of our wind chimes, or a light touch on my earlobe signal that your specter inhabits this place. It would be enough to console me if it were a promise that you would return.

It's not. You can't. You won't.

And so, I must breathe in air that keeps my heart beating, even though it has no use to me these days.

March 31, 2034
4:35 am

Note: I often craft pieces in the middle of the night. I type them into my phone and send them to myself via email. Sometimes, when I finally look at them, I have no recollection of writing them. Perhaps I can channel ideas when my barriers are broken down by fatigue? This is one of those mysterious essays. I showed it to my friend, and she remarked, "I love how you time travelled and have this writing from the future ... see date."

Whoa! I did not notice the typo. Maybe it was a missive from my future self?

IN MEMORIAM

I invite you to use these blank pages to add your own memories, drawings, and messages in honor of anyone you have adored.

Day 68

#2024bigyearproject

ABOUT THE AUTHOR

Jo-Jo Tabayoyong Murphy is a member of a rollicking, close-knit, supportive family. She also considers herself fortunate to have known many other warm groups through church, work, and hobbies. With a large circle, there are inevitable losses and additions. She has learned to accept that having relationships means facing life's most intense emotions. Writing about those experiences brings her clarity, peace, and many laughs.